EDINBURGH LIFE IN THE EIGHTEENTH CENTURY

THE LETTERS OF CAPTAIN TOPHAM AN OFFICER AND A GENTLEMAN

"EDINBURGH - Life in the Eighteenth & Nineteenth Centuries"

Published by Lang Syne Publishers Ltd., 45 Finnieston Street, Glasgow G3 8JU.
Printed by Dave Barr Print, 45 Finnieston Street, Glasgow G3 8JU.

© LANG SYNE PUBLISHERS LTD. 1989.

First published 1989. Reprinted 1994

ISBN N0. 1 85217 003 4

FRONT COVER: The bustle of Libberton's Wynd with Burns Tavern in the foreground.

BACK COVER: The New Assembly Hall in The Royal Mile.

All engravings courtesy of Mr John Nelson, Print Seller, Edinburgh.

INTRODUCTION

This unique book presents a fascinating picture of Edinburgh life two centuries ago through letters written by Captain Edward Topham, an English officer who spent six months living in the capital in 1775.

Educated at Eton and at Trinity College Cambrige, he obtained a Commission in the Guards and eventually rose to the rank of major.

Topham was a literary figure of not inconsiderable note in his time and owned a newspaper called The World.

After selling it he returned to the family seat in Yorkshire to spend the days quietly with his three daughters.

Part two of the book is an edited reprint of Henry Grey Graham's account of Edinburgh published in 1899 in "The Social Life of Scotland in the Eighteenth Century." He paints a fascinating picture of a town where everybody knew everybody else and all classes lived side by side in the teeming wynds. Taverns and oyster cellars were popular places of entertainment, yet the theatre and libraries were frowned upon by the Kirk which ruled over peoples' lives with a rod of iron. The Union of Parliaments had stripped Edinburgh of much of its former glory from 1707 but by the end of the century the capital was once again experiencing better days.

Description of the town in 1775

The situation of Edinburgh is probably as extraordinary an one as can well be imagined for a metropolis. The immense hills, on which great part of it is built, though they make the views uncommonly magnificent, not only in many places render it impassable for carriages, but very fatiguing for walking. The principal or great street runs along the ridge of a very high hill, which, taking its rise from the palace of Holyrood House, ascends, and not very gradually, for the length of a mile and a quarter, and after opening a spacious area, terminates in the Castle. On one side, as far as the eye can reach, you view the sea, the port of Leith, its harbour and various vessels, the river of Forth, the immense hills around, some of which ascend above even the Castle; and on the other side you look over a rich and cultivated country, terminated by the dark, abrupt, and barren hills of the Highlands.

You have seen the famous street at Lisle, la Rue royale, leading to the port of Tournay which is said to be the finest in Europe, but which I can assure you is not to be compared either in length or breadth to the High Street at Edinburgh; and would they be at the expense of removing some buildings which obstruct the view, by being placed in the middle of the street, nothing could be conceived more magnificent. Not content, however, with this, they suffer a weekly market to be held, in which stalls are erected nearly the whole length of it, and make a confusion almost impossible to be conceived. All sorts of iron and copper ware are exposed to sale; here likewise the herb market is held, and the herb women, who are in no country either the most peaceable or the most cleanly beings upon earth, throw about the roots, stalks, &c, of the bad vegetables, to the great nuisance of the passengers.

The style of building here is much like the French: the houses, however, in general are higher, as some rise to twelve, and one in particular to thirteen storeys in height. But to the front of the street nine or ten storeys is the common run; it is the back part of the edifice which, by being built on the slope of an hill, sinks to that amazing depth, so as to form the above number. This mode of dwelling, though proper for the turbulent times to which it was adapted, has now lost its convenience; as they no longer stand in need of the defence from the castle, they no more find the benefit of being crowded together so near it.

The buildings are divided, by extremely thick partition walls, into large houses, which are here called lands, and each storey of a land is called a house. Every land has a common staircase, in the same manner as the inns of court in London, and houses in Paris; from whence, it is most probable, this custom was taken. This staircase must always be dirty, and is in general very dark and narrow. It has this advantage, however, that as they are all of stone, they have little to apprehend from fire, which, in the opinion of some, would more than compensate for every other disadvantage. As each house is occupied by a family, a land, being so large, contains many families; and I make no manner of doubt but that the High Street in Edinburgh is inhabited by a greater number of persons than any street in Europe. The ground floors and cellars are in general made use of for shops by the tradesmen; who here style themselves merchants, as in France; and the higher houses are possessed by the genteeler people.

In London, you know, such an habitation would not be deemed the most eligible, and many a man in such a situation would not be sorry to descend a little lower. The style of building here has given rise to different ideas: Some years ago a Scotch gentleman, who went to London for the first time, took the uppermost storey of a lodging house and was very much surprised to find what he thought the genteelest place in the whole at the lowest price. His friends who came to see him, in vain acquainted him with the mistake he had been guilty of. "He ken'd verra weel", he said, "what gentility was, and when he lived all his life in a sixth storey, he was not come to London to live upon the ground."

The merchants here, as in France, have the horrid custom of painting on the outside of their houses the figure of the commodity which is to be sold within; which, in this place, makes the oddest appearance you can conceive; for each storey, perhaps, from top to bottom, is chequered with ten thousand different forms and colours, that the whole resembles the stall of a fair, presenting at one view, the goods of a variety of shops. They are likewise remarkably fond of glaring colours, — as red, yellow, and blue, — on which the figures are painted in black. You would laugh to see a black quartern loaf directly over a black full-trimmed periwig of a professor, with a Cheshire cheese, and a rich firkin of butter, displayed in black greasiness under stays, petticoats, and child-bed linen.

The other principal streets are parallel to the High Street on the south side, at the bottom of the hill, and are called the Cowgate and Grassmarket. Tradition says, the Cowgate two hundred years ago was the polite part of the town, and in it were the houses of the nobility and the senators of the College of Justice; but, at present, the buildings are much inferior to those on the top of the hill. The original town has been fortified, is surrounded by a wall, and has nine ports. The buildings are all of them of stone of a brown cast.

From the right of the High Street you pass over a very long bridge to the New Town. Before this bridge was built you had a very steep hill to descend and to ascend, which was found extremely inconvenient. A subscription therefore was entered into to build one; and a most stupendous work it is indeed: it is thrown over this immense valley; and by having no water run under it, you have the whole effect of its height. From it you have a fine view up and down the vale, and the prospect through the middle arch is inconceivably beautiful. Not long ago a part of this bridge gave way, and many people who were upon it sunk into the chasm, and were buried in the ruins. Many others, who were likewise upon the bridge, saw the fate of their unfortunate companions without being able to assist them. All was terror and consternation; every one fled from this scene of death as fast as possible, expecting the bridge to sink under them at every step, and themselves to be crushed to pieces. When the bridge was cleared, and the general consternation had a little subsided, it was found that only a small part had given way; which they are now repairing and making stronger than ever. But so great was the fear it occasioned amongst all ranks of people, that many of them look upon it with terror even to this day, and make it an objection to residing in the New Town that they must necessarily pass over it.

The New Town has been built upon one uniform plan, which is the only means of making a city beautiful. Great part of this plan as yet remains to be executed, though they proceed as fast as their supplies of money will allow them. The rent of the houses in general amount to £100 per annum, or upwards, and are most of them let to the inhabitants by builders, who buy the ground, and make what advantage they can of it. The greatest part of the New Town is built after the manner of the English, and the houses are what they call here "houses to themselves." Though this mode of living, one would imagine, is much preferable to the former, yet such is the force of prejudice, that there are many people who prefer a little dark confined tenement on a sixth storey to the convenience of a whole house. One old lady fancies she should be lost if she was to get into such an habitation; another, that she should be blown away in going over the new bridge; and a third lives in the old style because she is sure that these new fashions can come to "nae gude." But different as these sentiments are as regard to living, they are not more different than the buildings themselves. In no town that I ever saw can such a contrast be found betwixt the ancient and modern architecture, or anything that better merits the observation of a stranger.

The pavement of the whole town is excellent; the granite, which long supplied London till Jersey and Guernsey robbed them of those advantages, is dug from the hills close to the town, and brought at very small expense. Maitland, in his history of the town, calls it 'grey marble'; but without disputing about the propriety of the name, every one must allow it the very best stone possible for the purpose. They finish it with an exactness which the London workmen are indifferent about, and which indeed London would not admit of, from the number of weighty carriages that continually go over it.

From the left of the High Street you pass down by a number of different alleys, or as they call them here, wynds and closes, to the different parts of the old town. They are many of them so very steep that it requires great attention to the feet to prevent falling; but so well accustomed are the Scotch to that position of body required in descending these declivities, that I have seen a Scotch girl run down them with great swiftness in pattens.

Watching and Cleaning of the City, with an Account of the City Guard and the "Cadies"

This town has long been reproached with many uncleanly customs. A gentleman who lately published his travels through Spain, says "that Madrid, some years ago, might have vied with Edinburgh in filthiness." It may probably be some pleasure to this author, and to those who read him, to learn that his remarks are now very erroneous. And although, from the unfavourable situation of the houses, it is amazing the inhabitants preserve any degree of decency; yet you rarely find, in the worst part of the town, an obscure lodging that has not some degree of neatness, and a certain simplicity about it, to make it comfortable.

The police set an example by being particularly careful of the cleanness of the streets, into which, as a common sewer, all the nuisances of the houses are emptied at a stated time in the night, on the ringing of a bell, and immediately removed by persons appointed for that purpose; and at the same time the reservoirs being set open, which are placed at certain intervals in the streets, carry everything away; so that in the morning the streets are so clean that foot passengers walk in the middle of them. But I cannot help observing the intolerable stench that is produced at this season of the night on the moving the tub of nastiness from each floor: such a concatenation of smells I never before was sensible of; it has been sometimes so powerful as to wake me, and prevent my sleeping till it was somewhat pacified.

If a stranger may be allowed to complain, it would be that in the wynds, which are very numerous, the dirt is sometimes suffered to remain two or three days without removal, and becomes offensive in more senses than one. The magistrates, by imposing fines and other punishments, have long put a stop to the throwing of anything from the windows into the open street; but as these alleys are unlighted, narrow, and removed from public view, they still continue these practices with impunity. Many an elegant suit of clothes has been spoiled; many a powdered, well-dresed macaroni sent home for the evening; and, to conclude this period, in Dr Johnson's own simple words, "many a full-flowing periwig moistened into flaccidity."

Such particulars, however, as these scarce merit observation — they are circumstances resulting from the peculiar inconvenience of the buildings, and not from the natural disposition of the Scotch, who love cleanliness and practise it. They lament the impropriety of these customs, and join in the laugh at the accidents they occasion.

An Englishman, who has passed much of his life in London, and who has been entertained every morning with some dreadful account of robbery or outrage committed the evening before, would be much surprised on coming here to find that he might go with the same security at midnight as at noonday. A man, in the course of his whole life, shall not have the fortune here to meet with a house-breaker, or even so much as a single foot-pad; and a woman shall walk along the streets at any hour in an evening, without being "broke in upon", as Tristram Shandy says, "by one tender salutation." At eleven o'clock all is quiet and silent; not so much as a watchman to disturb the general respose. Now and then at a late — or rather an early — hour of the morning, you hear a little party at the taverns amusing themselves by breaking the bottles and glasses; but this is all in good humour, and what the constable has no business with.

As I do not imagine this is owing to the peculiar dispositions of the Scotch — for human nature, when occasion presents itself, is, I take it, the same in all places — we must attribute it to the excellence of the police. The city guard, who I assure you are very terrible-looking men, and perform their exercises every day in the High Street, to show people what they can do, have their stations, during the whole night, in the street, to prevent any quarrels or disorders that may arise there. These are relieved by others in their turn, so that the duty is performed by all of them in succession.

This guard is of very old standing, and commanded at present by no less a person than the Provost of Edinburgh, who is generally a tradesman, and consequently much used to arms. But I can with great truth inform you, that the command has been vested in persons equally formidable for two centuries or more. In the year 1580, the Common Council of Edinburgh formed citizens into companies of fifty men each, and appointed burgesses of the best experience in martial affairs to command them; for, as the Act wisely says, "It hath been found by experience, in many countries, that it is not so much the multitude that overcometh, as the experience and skill of well-trained and exercised soldiers, seeing it is the knowledge of warfare that emboldeneth to fight." So the experienced burgesses led on this bold band of citizens as often as their skill was called for. At present, however, their great knowledge in warfare has not many opportunities of showing itself; and as they are chiefly used as a guard during the night time, their heroic deeds are unfortunately concealed from public view. To do them justice, however, they seldom sleep upon their posts, which is saying a great deal for men who are not kept awake by the fear of an enemy. But whether the extreme good order and regularity which is observed in the streets, and the very few robberies which are committed, are entirely owing to these military men or not, is rather difficult to determine. I believe there are other people of a more civil nature, who share with them the hardships as well as the honour of accomplishing so great a task. These are a set of men who are called in this country Cadies, and who have been formed many years into a society for their own emolument and the public good — a society which is probably as useful and extraordinary as ever existed. It is under particular regulations, and it requires some interest to become a member of it. It is numerous, and contains persons for every use and employment, who faithfully execute all commands at a very reasonable price. To tell you what these people do is impossible; for there is nothing almost which they do not do. They are the only persons who may truly be said to have attained universal knowledge, for they know every thing and every body; they even know sometimes what you do, better than you yourself. The moment a stranger comes into Edinburgh, they know it; how long he is to stay, whither he is going, where he comes from, and what he is. In regard to the police, this may be a convenience, otherwise it would be a great nuisance. A certain number of them stand all day long, and most of the night, at the Cross in the High Street, waiting for employment. Whoever has occasion for them has only to pronounce the word "Cadie", and they fly from all parts to attend the summons. Whatever person you want, they know immediately where he is to be found, while without them it would be very difficult to find anybody, on account of the great height of the houses, and the number of families in every building. Trust them with what sum of money you please, you are quite safe; they are obliged by the rules of their Order to make good everything they lose. A gentleman once sent one of these Mercuries with a letter enclosing bills for some hundred pounds; the man lost it, and the Society (who are responsible for these losses) restored the sum to the proprietor.

Nothing can reflect more honour on this City, than the safety in which every man finds himself and his property. An Englishman, who has his house broken open twenty times in his life, calls it his Castle; and though he is afraid of stirring out of doors after it is dark, he is continually boasting to you of his liberty, and the security of his person.

The police of Paris has long been a subject of general and deserved admiration. A man may pass through the streets there at any hour in an evening, with as little danger as he would in the middle of the day. It is by the same means as in Paris that the police in Edinburgh is so well observed, which otherwise, from its populousness, and the style of the buildings, is as much calculated to conceal villains as any city whatever.

No people in the world undergo greater hardships, or live in a worse degree of wretchedness and poverty, than the lower classes here; but though they are very poor, I believe, as a nation, they are very honest: at least, their dishonesty takes a different turn from that of the common people in England; it runs into that concealed line of acting which, under the mask of insinuation and hypocrisy, works its way gradually to the purpose it wishes to attain, and not into that open and avowed villainy which seeks a miserable and precarious subsistence at the hazard of life, and which, even in danger and death, discovers a fortitiude that ought to be the result of virtue alone.

The Bad Accommodation for Strangers

One can scarcely form in imagination the distress of a miserable stranger on his first entrance into this city, as there is no inn that is better than an alehouse, nor any accommodation that is decent, cleanly, or fit to receive a gentleman. On my first arrival, my companion and self, after the fatigue of a long day's journey, were landed at one of these stable-keepers (for they have modesty enough to give themselves no higher denomination) in a part of the town which is called the Pleasance; and on entering the house, we were conducted by a poor girl without shoes or stockings, and with only a single linsey-woolsey petticoat, which just reached half way to her ankles, into a room where about twenty Scotch drovers had been regaling themselves with whisky and potatoes. You may guess our amazement, when we were informed, "that this was the best inn in the metropolis — that we could have no beds, unless we had an inclination to sleep together, and in the same room with the company which a stage-coach had that moment discharged." Well, said I to my friend (for you must know that I have more patience on these occasions than wit on any other) there is nothing like seeing men and manners, perhaps we may be able to repose ourselves at some coffee-house. Accordingly, on inquiry, we discovered that there was a good dame by the Cross, who acted in the double capacity of pouring out coffee, or letting lodgings to strangers, as we were. She was easily to be found out; and with all the conciliating complaisance of a Maitresse d'Hotel, conducted us to our destined apartments;

which were indeed six storeys high, but so infernal to appearance, that you would have thought yourself in the regions of Erebus.

The truth of this, I will venture to say, you will make no scruple to believe, when I tell you, that in the whole we had only two windows, which looked into an alley five foot wide, where the houses were at least ten storeys high, and the alley itself was so sombre in the brightest sunshine, that it was impossible to see any object distinctly.

It is extremely strange that a city which is a thoroughfare into all Scotland, and now little inferior in politeness to London in many respects, should not be better furnished with conveniences for strangers, or have a public lodging-house where you can find tolerable entertainment. But it really has not; and I should hope ere long the pride or good sense of Scotland will so far prevail as to establish an hotel in some suitable part of the town to obviate the inconvenience of the want of these necessaries.

The Manners of the People and Nature of their Amusements

A man who visits this country, after having been in France, will find, in a thousand instances, the resemblance which there is betwixt these two nations. That air of mirth and vivacity, that quick and penetrating look, that spirit of gaiety which distinguishes the French, is equally visible in the Scotch. It is the character of the nation; and it is a very happy one, as it makes them disregard even their poverty. Where there is any material difference, I believe it may be attributed to the difference of their religion; for that same Catholic religion, to say the truth of it, is a most comfortable one. The article of absolution is certainly a blessed invention, and renders the spirits free and unclouded by placing all the burthen of our sins upon another man's back.

A poor Englishman goes fretting and groaning, and carrying his miserable face into all companies, as contagious as an epidemical disorder, without one soul to take compassion on him, or pity his weakness; and should he not have a wife or family at home who cannot avoid him, he finds no person who will bear his infirmities, or look as sad as he does, but is constrained to wander about an unsociable being, till the month of November, and the *maladie Angloise*, relieve him from his distress.

But though the Scotch have no absolution, they have something very like it — a superstitious reliance on the efficacy of going constantly to church. Many of them may be said to pass half their lives there; for they go almost without ceasing, and look as sorrowful at the time as if they were going, not only to bury their sins, but themselves. At other hours, they are as cheerful and as gay as possible; and, probably, from hence arises that ease, that spirit in their conversation, which charms in every company, and which is the life of every society. They see no harm in innocent familiarity. They think a frank and unrestrained behaviour the best sign of a good heart, and agree with Lord Shaftesbury, "that gravity is the very essence of imposture."

Whenever the Scotch of both sexes meet, they do not appear as if they had never seen each other before, or wished never to see each other again; they do not sit in sullen silence, looking on the ground, biting their nails, and at a loss what to do with themselves; and, if some one should be hardy enough to break silence, start as if they were shot through the ear with a pistol; but they address each other at first sight, and with an *impressement* that is highly pleasing; they appear to be satisfied with one another, or at least, if they really are not so, they have the prudence to conceal their dislike. To see them in perfection is to see them at their entertainments.

When dinners are given here, they are invitations of form. The entertainment of pleasure is their suppers, which resemble the *petit soupers* of France. Of these thay are very fond; and it is a mark of their friendship to be admitted to be of the party. It is in these meetings that the pleasures of society and conversation reign, when the restraints of ceremony are banished, and you see people really as they are: and I must say, in honour of the Scotch, that I never met with a more agreeable people, with more pleasing or more insinuating manners, in my life. These little parties generally consist of about seven or eight persons, which prevents the conversation from being particular, which it always must be in larger companies. During the supper, which continues some time, the Scotch ladies drink more wine than an English woman could well bear; but the climate requires it, and probably in some measure it may enliven their natural vivacity. After supper is removed, and they are tired of conversing, they vary the scene by singing, in which many of the Scotch excel. There is a plaintive simplicity in the generality of their songs, to which the words are extremely well adapted, and which, from the mouth of a pretty Scotch girl, is inconceivably attracting. You frequently feel the force of those very expressions, that at another time you would not understand, when they are sung by a young person whose inclinations and affections are frequently expressed in the terms made use of, and which the heart claims as its own. The eye, the whole countenance speak frequently as much as the voice; for I have sometimes found, that I had a very just idea of the tenor of a song, though I did not comprehend three words in the whole.

Formerly it was the custom for the bagpipe to play during their entertainments, and every family had their bard. In these songs were rehearsed the martial and heroic deeds of their ancestors, as incentives to their own courage; but in these piping times of peace, "our stern alarms" have changed to "merry meetings", and tales of love and gentleness have succeeded to those of war. Instead of the drowsy hum of a bagpipe, which would certainly have laid my noble courage asleep, the voice of some pretty girl claims your attention, which, in my opinion, is no bad change. Altogether, the entertainments which this country affords are by no means contemptible. We have an elegant Playhouse, and tolerable performers; assemblies, concerts, public gardens, and walks, card parties, and a hundred other diversions, which in some degree keep me from pining for your Festino, Bach's concert, or Almack's.

As the genius of any people is not more easily discovered in their serious moments, than when they give a loose to freedom and pleasure: so the Scotch nation is peculiarly characterised by the mode of their diversions. A sober, sedate elegance pervades them all, blended with an ease and propriety which delights, and is sure to meet with approbation. A Scotchman does not relax himself for amusements, as if to pass away the hour; he seems, even in the height of pleasure, busy and intent, and as he would do, were he about to gain some advantage. His diversions are not calculated to seduce the unwary, or recreate the idle, but to unbend the mind, without corrupting it. He seems as if in his infancy he had been taught to make learning his diversion, and was now reversing it, and making his diversion his study. But besides the public entertainments of this city, which are derived from company, the inhabitants have more resources of pleasure within themselves, than in many other places. The young people paint, draw, are fond of music, or employ their hours in reading and acquiring the accomplishments of the mind. Every boarding-school Miss has something of this kind to recommend her, and make her an agreeable companion: and instead of a little smattering of French, which is the highest ambition to attain in Queen Square, you find them in Edinburgh entertaining in conversation, sentimental, and well informed. The mode of education of the young ladies here is highly to be commended, and admirably calculated to make them good wives. Besides needlework, and those trifling arts, which are the principal of their instruction in England, the precepts of morality, virtue, and honour are taught them from their earliest infancy, whilst they are instructed to consider themselves as beings born for society, for more than outside appearance and transitory pleasure, and to attend to the knowledge of what is useful, rather than the economy of a tambour-frame. The ladies also who undertake this arduous task of instruction are persons much better qualified in general than in other countries. They likewise introduce them into the politest company, and give them a taste for elegant and proper amusements, that when they leave school, they are not only mistresses of those accomplishments which are necessary to command a family, but have the deportment and behaviour of experienced women of fashion. No ladies in Scotland ever murder the precious moments in what is called "work", which is neither entertainment nor profit, merely because they must have the appearance of doing something, whilst they see everyone employed around them. They let no minute escape without its respective office, which may be of utility to themselves or others, and after a proper sacrifice to reading and literature, gain instruction from society and conversation.

The married ladies of this city seldom entertain large sets of company, or have routs, as in London. They give the preference to private parties and conversaziones, where they play at cards for small sums, and never run the risk of being obliged to discharge a debt of honour at the expense of their virtue and innocence. They often frequent the theatre, and show great taste and judgment in the choice of plays, where Mr Digges performs a principal character.

As to exercise, they seldom ride on horseback; but find much pleasure in walking, to which the soil and country is peculiarly adapted, being dry, pleasant, and abounding in prospects, and romantic scenes. It is likewise customary for them to drive in their carriages to the sands at Leith and Musselburgh, and parade backwards and forwards, after the manner of Scarborough, and other public places of sea-bathing resort. For vivacity and agility in dancing, none excel the Scotch ladies;

their execution in reels and country-dances is amazing; and the variety of steps which they introduce, and the justness of their ear is beyond description. They are very fond also of minuets, but fall greatly short in the performance of them, as they are deficient in grace and elegance in their motions. Many of them play on the harpsichord and guitar, and some have music in their voices: though they rather love to hear others perform than play themselves.

I do not think the Scotch ladies are great proficients in the languages. They rarely attempt anything further than the French; which, indeed, they speak with great propriety, fluency, and good accent; but they make up for it by their accurate and just knowledge of their own. They talk very grammatically; are peculiarly attentive to the conformity of their words to their ideas, and are great critics in the English tongue. They chiefly read history, and plaintive poetry: but elegies and pastorals are their favourites. Novels and romances they feel, and admire; and those chiefly which are tender, sympathetic, soothing, or melancholy. Their hearts are soft and full of passion, and a well-told story makes a deep impression on them. Like virgin wax, a gentle heat mollifies their minds, which reflects the finest touches of art and sentiment.

Nor are the gentlemen in Edinburgh less rational in their diversions than the ladies. There is only one, in which I can censure their conduct: they pay rather too much respect to the divinity of Bacchus, and offer too copious libations at the shrine of that jovial deity. Their wines, indeed, of all kinds are excellent, and their climate not the most comfortable; so that some allowance ought to be made them in that respect. But as they are, they are by no means so intemperate as the Germans; and, perhaps, their appearing to me in the least intemperate, may be occasioned by my peculiar aversion to, and abstinence from all intoxicating liquors. I have neither taste to relish, nor head to bear them. I have no idea of a man extending the pleasure of drinking beyond thrift, or forcing in imagination, an appetite artificial and against nature.

The youths in this country are very manly in their exercises and amusements. Strength and agility seems to be most their attention. The insignificant pastimes of marbles, tops, &c, they are totally unacquainted with. The diversion which is peculiar to Scotland, and in which all ages find pleasure, is golf. They play at it with a small leathern ball, like a fives ball, and a piece of wood, flat on one side, in the shape of a small bat, which is fastened at the end of a stick of three or four feet long, at right angles to it. The art consists in striking the ball with this instrument into a hole in the ground in a smaller number of strokes than your adversary. This game has the superiority of cricket and tennis, in being less violent and dangerous, but in point of dexterity and amusement, by no means to be compared with them. However, I am informed that some skill and nicety are necessary to strike the ball to the proposed distance and no farther, and that in this there is a considerable difference in players. It requires no great exertion and strength, and all ranks and ages play at it. They instruct their children in it as soon as they can run alone, and grey hairs boast their execution. As to their other diversions, they dance, play at cards, love shooting, hunting, and the pleasures of the field, but are proficient in none of them. When they are young, indeed, they dance, in the manner of their country, extremely well; but afterwards (to speak in the language of the turf) they train off, and are too robust and muscular to possess either grace or agility.

I am sorry to say the hazard table is in high fashion and estimation. There are clubs in Edinburgh who may vie with White's or Almack's. But the misfortune is, there is a deficiency of ready money, which obliges them to keep books, by which they transfer their debts to one another. This renders it both inconvenient and troublesome to strangers to engage them: for if you lose, their necessity compels them to demand immediate payment; and, on the contrary, if you chance to be successful, they refer you to twenty different people before you can expect your money; and you have reason to bless your stars if ever you obtain it. I do not know anything so disgusting, or against the grain of politeness, as being obliged to dun a gentleman for a game debt; but here it is absolutely necessary: if you do not, you play without the least chance of being a winner.

The Dress of the better sort of Inhabitants

The women here do not so readily adopt any trifling fashion from London. They conform themselves much more to the manners and taste of Paris, with which they have as constant a communication as with England. The ladies in Edinburgh dress, in general, with more elegance, and in a way better accommodated to their persons, size, and shape, than most of the European nations; whilst they are peculiarly attentive to the nature of their climate and seasons, as well as to their age, after the manner of the French. You never see the mortifying spectacle of an old woman displayed in all the show and vanity of a boarding-school Miss; or the widowed wife of nineteen assuming the air and dress of an ancient married matron, in order to adapt herself to the age of a decrepit and peevish husband. In a morning, also, their dress is equally becoming; their *deshabile* is never negligent and loose, but neat and plain, with a degree of smartness and elegance; and a genius for dress even then discovers itself, just as you may see the masterly strokes of a poet in two or three unpremeditated extempore verses. But I wish I could say as much for the men: they neither take so much care of their persons or appearance, nor have they half the taste in dress that the ladies have, who choose the most becoming fashions from London and Paris, and form one of their own, more graceful, perhaps, than either. But the gentlemen neither know how, nor are studious of setting off their figure to advantage. In the politest assemblies in this city you rarely see a gentleman well dressed. In those that think themselves the best there is always some deficiency, whilst you will not find one lady without every assistance of ornament and art; and an ill-dressed lady is as great a novelty as an ill-bred one.

But however they may be indebted to external show, or whatever they may have borrowed from the French, they derive none of their beauty from paint, nor have they had folly enough to imitate that nation in this absurd fashion. Indeed, neither their colour nor complexion stand in need of it; for I know not where they will find their equals in either. The women's hair is either a dark brown or perfectly red, which I esteem a very beautiful colour, and is that which in ancient times was so admired, received the appellation of golden, and was given by way of distinction to a Pallas or a Juno. I am sorry to say the ladies here often conceal it by powder, making no difference between it and that sandy-coloured red, which of all hair is the most disagreeable and unbecoming. In most respects they dress their hair with great elegance and propriety, in no extremes, neither too elevated nor too depressed, but in that just-proportioned medium, which is always the result of taste and judgment. As to hoops, they seldom use them, and add very little to their height by the heels of their shoes.

Many of the ladies marry at fifteen, and many of the married ladies at twenty-five, look no younger than some of the English women at forty. This early loss of beauty may, in some measure, proceed from the negligence of their persons the moment they are married, as if, on that important day, all future desires of pleasing were to be closed, and one dark cloud of constancy and indifference was to shade the whole scene.

The gentlemen, after the custom of the French, wear their hair in bags, especially the advocates and professors of the College, who commonly dress in black. With respect to clothes, as I said before, I cannot speak in great praise of them; and they have the worst tailors, perhaps, in the world.

The Theatre

Edinburgh, which has been for a long time without trade or company, a mere mass without spirits, seems to be animated with new life. The classes in the College are sitting, the terms are begun, the scenes of diversion are opened, and all is business, pleasure, and confusion.

This metropolis is said to be very gay; and, if I may judge from the little specimen I have already had of it, reports say nothing but the truth. The concerts have received the assistance of a new singer from London, the assemblies are opened for the reception of those who choose to dance, and the theatrical heroes have already opened their campaign. As yet, I believe, they have had but few spectators, as the genteel people here fix one day for beginning to partake of these amusements, and are so very polite, that they never go before that day on any account.

The present Theatre is situated at the end of the New Bridge in the New Town, and on the outside is a plain structure like most others of the same nature. It was built by the subscription of a number of gentlemen, who let it originally to a manager for four hundred pounds a year. Mr Ross was the first person who took it, and his name was inserted in the patent, which made him manager as long as he chose. A few years ago plays were not in that repute at Edinburgh they now are. The ministers, zealous for the good of their flock, preached against them, and the poor players were entirely routed: they have now, however, once more taken the field, and the clergy leave them to their ungodliness.

The Theatre is of an oblong form, and designed after the manner of foreign ones. I do not know its exact dimensions; but at three shillings (which is the price of admittance into the pit and boxes) it is capable of containing about one hundred and thirty pounds. The pit seems considered here as the *Parterre* in the French theatre, into which gentlemen go who are not sufficiently dressed for the boxes. On very crowded nights the ladies sometimes sit here, and then that part of it is divided by a partition. The ornaments are few, and in an unaffected plain style, which, on the whole, has a very elegant appearance. It is lighted with wax, and the scenery is well painted; though they do not excel in those *jeux de theatre* which please and astonish the common people in London. The whole of their machinery is luckily very bad; and, therefore, much to the credit of their understandings, they have seldom any Harlequin entertainments: I have only seen one or two since I came here; but the *deceptio visus*, if such it could be called, was so miserable, that the poor players themselves seemed ashamed of it.

The upper galleries, or, as they very obligingly term them in London, "the Gods", seem here very compassionate divinities. You sometimes hear the murmurings of displeasure at a distance; but they never rain down oranges apples, &c, on the heads of the unfortunate actors. They suffer them very quietly "to strut their hour upon the stage", and if then they dislike them, "they are literally heard no more."

It is probable, that from an attention to these small and seemingly trivial circumstances, that you discover more of the real manners of a people, than from the greater and more public events in life, where the passions are naturally excited, and men act under a disguise. A boisterous fellow in England, who thinks it a part of his privilege to do what he thinks proper, provided neither the laws nor *magna carta* forbid it, when he takes a dislike to an actor, drives all the players off the stage, puts an end to the performance, and insults the whole audience. A Frenchman, and a Scotchman, whom an arbitrary government in one instance, and the remains of it in the other, has softened and refined, keep their quarrels to themselves, consider the poor players as incapable of resistance, and show their dislike to them only by not applauding them.

The Mode of Conducting Funerals

I know no place where you behold more frequent funerals than in this city, and they are conducted with a silence and a solemnity which makes sorrow appear still more dismal. On these occasions, in England, you know, no distress is seen; for, as the afflicted hire others to mourn for them, it cannot be supposed that people should be affected by distresses which are nothing to them. An Englishman seems to carry with him the same desires out of life, which he had in it; and as all his pleasure was centred in going post, you frequently meet his hearse at full gallop, as if, after having been in a hurry all his lifetime, it was decreed he should find no rest even in death.

In this place, instead of applying to an undertaker for a group of grim figures, and dismal faces, they send a card, as the French do, to all the persons of their acquaintance, desiring their attendance at the funeral. If the people who are invited do not really feel sorrow, in compliment at least they affect to do so: and therefore, you are not shocked with any ill-timed mirth or outward signs of insensibility. They all dress themselves at these meetings in a suit of black, which has something in it peculiarly mournful: all the nearest relations, besides putting on weepers, which are common with us, fix a long piece of muslin to the collar of the shirt, that hangs down before as far as the middle to the waist. They continue in this fashion all the time they wear their first mourning, and sometimes the excess of their grief is in proportion to these pieces of muslin.

In the funerals of the lower classes of people, the procession is always on foot. The coffin is carried by four people, the minister walks before it, and all the friends and relations follow. They proceed with a slow, solemn pace to the kirk; and as the relationship extends itself a great way in this country, a whole street is sometimes nearly filled with this sable procession.

Persons of higher rank are carried in hearses; but with none of that ostentatious pomp and ceremony which is so frequent, and generally so ridiculous in England. The vanity of people in this country dies with them. You are never astonished with a display of which they can be no longer sensible, and from whence no gratification can be derived, but one of the most melancholy and disgusting nature: a hearse, followed by a mourning coach, is all the parade that you see; and if a man has done nothing in life worth remembering, he has no chance of making himself immortal by his funeral. The undertakers seem the only people who suffer by all this humility; they neither find people to mourn, nor plumes of feathers, nor carriages, nor any of those *insignia mortis,* which few people would think of having, could they only see the bill.

There is one instance of politeness which the Scotch show each other, and which, as far as mere ceremonial can be agreeable, is certainly so; whenever a relation of any family dies, the first visit made to them by their friends and even acquaintances, is always made in mourning, as if to sympathise with their distress. This piece of form they observe with great care; and a person would be thought a strange creature who should go dressed in colours to the house of mourning. This custom is never repeated. From these civilities, and the frequent mournings which the numerous relationships occasion, many families are almost constantly clothed in black; and on entering a large room full of company, one would sometimes imagine that an epidemical disorder was raging in the town, and that every one of them had lost some near relation. But whether it is from the constant habit of mourning that the occasion of it loses in some measure its effect, or that they are a nation of philosophers, they do not appear to me to feel with all that lively and tender sensitivity, which is visible in some countries. They weep for a little time, then they begin to think of something fashionable for a mourning dress, and everything goes on as before. The widows, indeed, put on so very sorrowful an appearance, and wrap themselves so entirely in black, that one would imagine they had devoted the rest of their lives to melancholy, and never intend to take another husband. But yet, in spite of all this, many of them do.

An Execution

I was this morning a witness to one of the most solemn and mournful of all spectacles, the execution of a criminal. Death is always affecting; but it becomes still more moving when we behold a poor wretch sacrificed to the injured laws of his country.

In Scotland, and I mention it to its honour, there is, on these unhappy occasions, much more solemnity and decency observed than in Paris. The lenity of the laws here makes it necessary that a man shall be "habit and repute" a thief, before he can be condemned to die for theft; and therefore, executions, except for murder, are very uncommon. This man had already been twice convicted and pardoned; so that there was no room for intercession to the King's mercy; nor was there the least hope of his amendment, as he was near sixty years old, had spent the whole of his life in a series of repeated thefts, and as he advanced in age, had advanced likewise in iniquity.

The town of Edinburgh, from the amazing height of its buildings, seems peculiarly formed to make a spectacle of this kind solemn and affecting. The houses, from the bottom up to the top, were lined with people, every window crowded with spectators to see the unfotunate man pass by. At one o'clock the City Guard went to the door of the Tolbooth, the common gaol here, to receive and conduct their prisoner to the place of execution, which is always in the Grass Market, at a very great distance from the prison. All the remaining length of the High Street was filled with people, not only from the town itself, but the country around, whom the novelty of the sight had brought together. On the Guard knocking at the door of the Tolbooth, the unhappy criminal made his appearance. He was dressed in a white waistcoat and breeches, usual on these occasions, bound with black ribands, and a night-cap tied with the same. His white hairs, which were spread over his face, made his appearance still more pitiable. Two clergymen walked on each side of him, and were discoursing with him on subjects of religion. The executioner, who seemed ashamed of the meanness of his office, followed, muffled up in a great coat, and the City Gaurds, with their arms ready, marched around him. The criminal, whose hands were tied behind him, and the rope about his neck, walked up the remaining part of the street. It is the custom in this country for a criminal to walk to the gallows, which has something much more decent in it than being thrown into a cart, as in England, and carried, like a beast, to slaughter. The slow, pensive, melancholy step of a man in these circumstances has something in it that seems to accord with affliction, and affects the mind forcibly with its distress. It is the pace which a man in sorrow naturally falls into.

When the criminal had descended three parts of the hill which leads to the Grass Market, he beheld the crowd waiting for his coming, and the instrument of execution at the end of it. He made a short stop here, naturally shocked at such a sight, and the people seemed to sympathise with his affliction. When he reached the end, he recalled his resolution; and, after passing some time in prayer with the clergyman, and once addressing himself to the people, he was turned off, and expired. So great is the abhorrence of the office of executioner in this country, that the poor wretch is obliged to be kept three or four days in prison, till the hatred of the mob has subsided, and his act is forgotten.

PART TWO

Why Edinburgh hated the Union of Parliaments

The height of Edinburgh's glory was before the Union of 1707, in the days when meetings of the Scots Parliament drew to the capital nobles and persons of quality from every county, when periodically the city was full of the richest, most notable, and best-bred people in the land, and the dingy High Street and Canongate were brightened by gentlemen in their brave attire, by ladies rustling in their hoops, brocade dresses, and brilliant coloured plaids, by big coaches gorgeous in their gilding, and lackeys splendid in their livery. For the capital of a miserably poor country, Edinburgh had then a wonderful display of wealth and fashion. After 1707 all this was sadly changed. "There is the end of an auld sang", said Lord Chancellor Seafield in jest, whether light or bitter, when the Treaty of Union was concluded; but it was a "song" that lingered long in the hearts of those who knew it well, associated with a long eventful history, and leaving many regretful memories behind it. No more was the full concourse of men and ladies of high degree to make society brilliant with the chatter of right honourable voices, the glint of bright eyes from behind the masks, the jostling of innumerable sedan-chairs in the busy thoroughfare, where nobles and caddies, judges and beggars, forced their way with equal persistency. Instead of the throng of 145 nobles and 160 commoners, who often with their families and attendants filled the town with life and business, there went to Westminster the sixteen representative peers and sixty members of Parliament, travelling reluctantly and tediously and expensively by the wretched roads, and lodging in London at ruinous charges — and all for what? To find themselves obscure and unhonoured in the crowd of English society and the unfamiliar intrigues of English politics, where they were despised for their poverty, ridiculed for their speech, sneered at for their manners, and ignored in spite of their votes by the Ministers and Government.

No wonder the Union was specially unpopular in Edinburgh, for it deprived the city of national dignity, carried from citizens their fashions, and spoiled their trade. A gloom fell over the Scots capital: society was dull, business was duller still, the lodgings once filled with persons of quality were left empty — many decayed for want of tenants, some fell almost into ruin. For many a year there was little social life, scanty intellectual culture, and few traces of business enterprise. Gaiety and amusement were indulged in only under the censure of the Church and the depressing air of that gloomy piety which held undisputed and fuller sway when the influence of rank and fashion no longer existed to counteract it.

Gardy loo! The not so sweet Flowers of Edinburgh

The town, all enclosed within the city walls, chiefly consisted of one long street — Canongate and High Street — that stretched a mile long from Holyrood to the Castle, with the low-lying parallel Cowgate. From this main thoroughfare branched off innumerable closes and wynds, in which lived a dense population, gentle and simple. There was something impressive in the houses towering to ten to twelve stories in height of that extended street, though its continuity was then broken midway by the Netherbow Port — the Temple Bar of Edinburgh — with its huge iron gateway. There was picturesqueness in the houses, whose wooden-faced gables were turned to the streets, the projecting upper story making piazzas below. But the few visitors from England were impressed far more by its dirt and dinginess than by its quaint beauty, by the streets which were filthy, the causeways rugged and broken, the big gurgling gutters in which ran the refuse of a crowded population, and among which the pigs poked their snouts in grunting satisfaction for garbage. By ten o'clock each night the filth collected in each household was poured from the high windows, and fell in malodorous plash upon the pavement, and not seldom on unwary passers-by. At the warning call of "Gardy loo" *(Gardez l'eau)* from servants preparing to outpour the contents of stoups, pots, and cans, the passengers beneath would agonisingly cry out, "Haud yer hand"; but too often the shout was unheard or too late, and a drenched periwig and besmirched three-cornered hat were borne dripping and ill-scented home. At the dreaded hour when the domestic abominations were flung out, when the smells (known as the "flowers of Edinburgh") filled the air, the citizens burnt their sheets of brown paper to neutralise the odours of the outside, which penetrated the rooms within. On the ground all night the dirt and ordure lay awaiting the few and leisurely scavengers, who came nominally at seven o'clock next morning with wheel-barrows to remove it. But ere that morning hour the streets were becoming thronged, for people rose and business began early, and the shopkeepers, treading cautiously amidst the filth and over the teeming gutters, had set forth to open their booths. Worst of all was the Sunday, when strict piety forbade all work, deeming that street-cleansing was neither an act of necessity nor one of mercy, and required the dirt to remain till Monday morning.

While high overhead towered the houses in the air, many in the Lawnmarket had pillared piazzas on the ground floor, under which were the open booths where merchants showed their wares. Others spread them on the pavement in front of their shops, and in the middle of the street near St Giles were open spaces, where on stalls the special crafts displayed their goods — woollen stuffs, linen, or pots — for the shops were too small and too obscure to accommodate or show off the modest stores their owners possessed. In the second or third flat of the Luckenbooths — a row of tall narrow houses standing in front of St Giles and blocking the High Street — the best tradesmen had their shops, at a rental of which the very highest rate was £15, and not a few of these shopkeepers, notwithstanding their humble rooms and slender stock of goods, were members of high Scots county families. Others in good position had their business in cellars or little chambers on the basement, to which the customers descended by worn stone steps, and in which there was little space to turn and little light to see by. Few goods were kept in stock, and the customer for silk, cloth, or jewellery must give his order betimes, and patiently wait till it came its slow course from London by waggon, or from Holland or Flanders by the boat to Leith three months afterwards.

The wynds and 'dirty luggies'

In the flats of the lofty houses in wynds or facing the High Street the populace dwelt, who reached their various lodgings by the steep and narrow "scale" staircases, which were really upright streets. On the same building lived families of all grades and classes, each in its flat on the same stair — the sweep and caddie in the cellars, poor mechanics in the garrets, while in the intermediate stories might live a noble, a lord of session, a doctor, or city minister, a dowager countess, or writer; higher up, over their heads, lived shopkeepers, dancing masters, or clerks. The rents of these mansions varied curiously in the same close, or same stair, from the cellars and garrets paying £12 Scots (18s) to the best-class chambers paying £300 Scots (£20). But the common rent of a gentleman's dwelling in the

ST GILES AND HIGH STREET

BAKEHOUSE CLOSE CANONGATE

THE FAMOUS WHITE HORSE INN

OLD VILLAGE OF BROUGHTON

THE JAIL AND GOVERNOR'S HOUSE from back of Canongate

THE WEST BOW

ROYAL EXCHANGE, HIGH STREET

SURGEON'S SQUARE

EDINBURGH CASTLE

OLD FISH MARKET CLOSE FROM THE COWGATE

JOHN KNOX'S HOUSE

first half of the century was £8 or £10 a year. Lord President Dundas used to say that even when his income was 20,000 merks (£1000), he lived in a house at £100 Scots (£8:6:8) and had only two roasts a week. But living was then plain, for incomes were small; a minister in his city charge in the middle of the century and a professor in the University were thought well off with £100 or £130 a year, while a lord of session had a salary of £500. The dark, narrow stairs, with their stone steps worn and sloping with traffic, were filthy to tread on; and on reaching the flat where lodged an advocate in extensive practice, eyes and nose encountered at the door the "dirty luggies" in which were deposited the contents which, as St Giles' bells rang out ten o'clock, were to be precipitated from the windows. On the door, instead of a bell or knocker, was a "risp", which consisted of a notched or twisted rod of iron with a ring attached, which the visitor rasped up and down upon the notches till the door was opened by a maidservant, probably with neither shoes nor stockings.

The rooms within were entered from a narrow, ill-lighted lobby, and were low-ceilinged, deriving light from the spare windows which long before sunset had faded into gloom. Sometimes in the public rooms there were signs of dignity and art, in the elaborately stuccoed ceiling, the finely carved massive marble mantelpiece, the walls oak-panelled or covered with gilt leather, with landscape panels from the hand of "old Norrie", the decorator; but usually the rooms were plain and poor, crammed with furniture for which there was no space. The accommodation in a mansion of high class would be six rooms, including the kitchen. Far on in the century in the public rooms there were beds, concealed during day by curtains. Campbell of Succoth, an eminent lawyer, lived in his flat in St James' Court, where his clerks worked in a little closet without a fire-place, and when the Duke of Argyll and other big clients dined with him, they were received in Mr and Mrs Campbell's bedroom. Partly from economy, partly from lack of space, the staff of servants was extremely limited, for often one — and there was no accommodation for more than two — did the work of the household on a wage of 20s a year and a gown.

Serving maids slept in kitchen drawers!

In the house of a gentleman who luxuriously kept his carriage the servant slept under a dresser in the kitchen, while his man slept over the stable; and in a flat occupied by an eminent judge the maid slept as best she could in a drawer in the kitchen which was shut up during the day. Owing to the scantiness of space, the nurse and children would probably sleep in the study, if such existed, the beds being removed during the day, when the lord of session worked over his charges or the nobleman saw his friends, while the lady in her bedroom was entertaining her guests at tea.

The air in these low rooms was not extremely fresh, especially when it came from those windows which opened into fetid closes or wynds, which were so narrow that the inhabitants could converse easily and exchange friendly cups of tea with their neighbours on the other side. The long precipitous stairs were crowded all day long with men, women, and children belonging to the various flats passing up and down — masons, judges, dancing masters, countesses, barbers, and advocates, all encountered each other in the narrow passage. Besides the residents there was the stream of porters carrying coals, the Musselburgh fishwives with their creels, the sweeps, the men and women conveying the daily supply of water for each flat, barbers' boys with retrimmed wigs, the various people bent on business or on pleasure, on errands and visits for the several landings, all jostling unceremoniously as they squeezed past one another. It was no easy task for brilliantly dressed ladies to crush their hoops, four or five yards in circumference, up the scale-stairs, or to keep them uncontaminated by the dirt abounding on the steps. So confined were some of the stairs that it was sometimes impossible, when death came, to get the coffin down; and when a passage was too narrow for that purpose, the power was possessed by legal servitude for the tenant of a house so situated to get entry through the adjacent house, and bring the coffin down its more commodious stair.

The hours for rising were early in these old times, and the city was astir by five o'clock in the morning. Before the St Giles' bells had sounded seven the shops were open, the shutters were flung back on their hinges, and over the half-door the tradesmen were leaning, chatting to their neighbours, and receiving the latest news; while citizens walked down to the little post-office, situated up a stair, to get the letters just brought in by the post-runner from Glasgow or Aberdeen, instead of waiting till they were distributed through the town by the single letter-carrier of the city, or even the three carriers who were installed in 1717. In the taverns the doctors were seeing their patients. Up till 1713 the celebrated physician Dr Archibald Pitcairn, was to be found in the dingy underground cellar, called from its darkness the "groping office", near St Giles'. Early every morning, by six o'clock, President Dalrymple had seen his agent, and gone over a dozen cases before his breakfast. Eight o'clock was the breakfast hour, with its substantial meal of mutton, collops, and fowl, with libations of ale, and sometimes sack, claret, or brandy — tea not being used at that meal till about 1730. The citizen shut his shop, or left his wife to tend it, when the St Giles' bells rang at half-past eleven — a well-known sound which was known as the "gill-bells", because each went to his favourite tavern to take his "meridian", consisting of a gill of brandy, or a tin of ale. Little these citizens heeded the music-bells, which meanwhile overhead were playing the bright charming tunes to which wiser folk were all listening. The dinner hour was at one o'clock till 1745, when it was changed to two, though the humbler shopkeepers dined at twelve. The wonted fare in winter was broth, salt beef, boiled fowls; for only the wealthy could afford to get fresh beef at high prices until the summer, when the arrival of any supply of beef for sale was announced in the streets by the bellman.

Sedan chairs and snuff

By two o'clock all citizens wended their way down their respective stairs to their places of business, reopened the doors, and hung up the key on a nail on the lintel — a practice which afforded the notorious burglar, Deacon Brodie, in 1780, opportunities of taking impressions of the keys on putty. By the early afternoon the streets were crowded, for into the main thoroughfare the inhabitants of the city poured. Later in the century an Englishman describes the scene: "So great a crowd of people are nowhere else confined in so small a space, which makes their streets as much crowded every day as others are at a fair." There were few coaches, fortunately, in the narrow steep streets; but there were sedan-chairs swaying in all directions, borne by Highland porters, spluttering Gaelic execrations on all those who impeded their progress. There were ladies in gigantic hoops sweeping the sides of the causeway, their head and shoulders covered with their gay silken plaids, scarlet and green, their faces with complexions heightened by patches, and concealed by black velvet masks which were held close by a string, whose buttoned end was held by the teeth. In their hands they bore huge green paper fans to ward off the sun; by their side hung the little bags which held the snuff they freely used; their feet shod in red shoes, with heels three inches high, with which they tripped nimbly on the steep decline and over filthy places. There were stately old ladies, with their pattens on feet and canes in hand, walking with precision and dignity; judges with their wigs on head and hats under their arm; advocates in their gowns on way to the courts in Parliament House; ministers in their blue or gray coats, bands, wigs, and three-cornered hats. At the Cross (near St Giles') the merchants assembled to transact business, and to exchange news and snuff-boxes; while physicians, lawyers, and men about town met them as at an open-air club, and joined citizens in the gossip of the city.

At four o'clock the ladies had their refection, for the "four hours" all over Scotland, and with all ranks, was a necessary refreshment of the day. In the largest houses the hostess received her visitors in the drawing-room; but in smaller flats she was obliged, as in the country, to see them in her bedroom. Till about 1720 ladies had drunk their ale or claret; but when tea came into vogue that beverage became a necessity, and wine was reserved for the gentlemen. On the mahogany tea-table were liliputian cups for the expensive beverage, with spoons all numbered, lest in the confusion, when every cup was returned before a fresh helping was served to any, the wrong cup should be given; fine linen napkins were handed to each guest to preserve their gowns from speck and spot. By eight o'clock all visitors had gone, for the supper hour had come; the maids had arrived with the pattens for the elderly ladies, and lanterns to light their mistresses to their homes in the dark wynds and stairs. When citizens began their copious suppers, they ate and drank till late, and guests departed not too soberly, while the servant guided their meandering footsteps and held a candle or lantern to light them to the "mouth" of the close.

Kirk's relentless hunt for sinners and scandals

The amusements of the town during the early part of the century were neither varied nor lively. For this dullness and social sombreness the Church and popular piety were responsible. All gaiety was looked on with grim censure. Kirk-Sessions uttered anathemas against all worldly pleasure, exercised tyrannical sway over every day of the week and over every action of the people. Sabbath was the special day when every act and moment of existence were watched; the doing of any work, the indulgence of the slightest recreation, was forbidden; the "vaguing" or loitering in the streets or on the Castle hill, the mere "gazing idlely" out of the windows, was a subject of condemnation and occasion of threats of discipline by Kirk-Sessions, and of fine by magistrates. To secure the perfect observance of the Lord's Day, the bailies had "seizers" or compurgators, appointed at the instance of the Church, who took hold of any one "during sermons" who dared to neglect divine service and forthwith reported him to the general Kirk-Session. In the evening the patrol watched the streets, which usually in those days were deserted like a city of the dead; followed any belated passenger's echoing footsteps, peered down wynds, looked up stairs for any lurking transgressors of the law of Mount Sinai. The "kirk treasurer", appointed by the Session, whose very name was at once a subject of mockery and an object of terror, was ever on the alert for scandals and culprits that brought in fines and fees. The voice of the Church was stern against the barbers who on Sabbath furtively carried the gentlemen's wigs all ready trimmed for worship, or went to shave them into tidiness. This demand for the services of barbers made that craft one of the largest and most prosperous in the community; for gentlemen, instead of "barbourising" themselves, to use the expression of the day, were dependent on their servants or their wig-makers to shave their heads.

Every pleasure of the week-day was watched and reprobated as grimly as were all desecrations of the Sabbath — the theatre, dancing, the club. The last was a source of horror to the pious in the early part of the century, as being the scene of hideous orgies, and resort of those who ridiculed the Kirk, and the Whigs without any principles on either Church or politics. The names that these re-unions bore — the "Sulphur Club", the "Hell-Fire Club", the "Horn Club", the "Demireps" — had a dare-devil and dare-kirk sound; the free talk of their members, their ribald verses, their blaspheming songs, as wildly rumoured abroad, became the scandal of the town, while the iniquities of the Hell-Fire Club were considered past mention.

Why theatre was condemned as evil

There was no theatre for a long while in Edinburgh; but occasionally travelling companies came from England, — "filling up our cup of sin", groaned the ministers.

In 1736 Allan Ramsay was anxious to add to his many occupations of ex-wigmaker, poet, and librarian, that of theatre-manager, and built a play-house in Carrubber's Close, which was opened only to be summarily shut under the influence of clergy and magistrates. In vain the versatile little citizen brought his complaint for loss of money before the Court of Session; he got only the subtle verdict that "though he had been damaged, he had not been injured." The career of the drama in Edinburgh was precarious and chequered. Denounced by the ministers, discouraged by the magistrates, the theatre received no licence. But, evasive of the law, plays were performed in the Taylor's Hall, and, to escape the legal penalty, were advertised as being given "gratis" after a concert. The entertainment was announced as "a concert of musick with a play between the acts", and the prudest might go and enjoy Vanbrugh's *Provoked Husband* and Wycherley's unsavoury *Country Wife* under guise of innocently listening to Corelli's sonatas. It was in 1756 that the town was delighted and the Church horrified by the performance of the tragedy of *Douglas* from the pen of Mr John Home, minister of Athelstaneford, given in the presence of several brother ministers of the Gospel. The Edinburgh Presbytery drew up its exhortation that "all within its bounds discourage the illegal and dangerous entertainments of the stage, and restrain those under their influence from frequenting such seminaries of vice and folly." Other Presbyteries censured or suspended ministers for their profane audacity in attending such improper places, and the delinquents received their rebukes solemnly in public and laughed at them heartily in private.

In spite of all the excitement of the godly, the very fact that ministers and elders dared to countenance a stage play showed that the old bigotry was beginning to lose its hold. The people thronged the play-house till the Church in despair ceased to fulminate at the pit of a theatre as leading to the pit that is bottomless, and at last, in 1764, a theatre was licensed and set up on a field which had been the scene of Whitfield's fervent religious meetings.

Gentlemen had their other amusements on which, fortunately, the religious world laid no embargo. They had their golf, their archery, their horse-races on Leith sands — which the most scrupulous magistrates did not hesitate to encourage by presenting cups as prizes. There were also the less praiseworthy cock-pits resorted to by high and low, eagerly; and, later in the century, might be seen Deacon Brodie, fresh from committing a burglary, and Henry Mackenzie, just come from inditing a teaful scene of his "Man of Feeling", watching their "mains". Strange to say, the clergy who were ready to denounce all carnal pleasure, even in the decorous form of a minuet, uttered no complaint against the coarse and demoralising sport of cock-fighting. Why this ecclesiastical reticence? Obviously because every one had been accustomed to that sport at every parish school. Every minister in his boyish days had himself indulged in it, when on Fastern Eve or Shrove Tuesday he had proudly brought his own favourite cock under his arm to pit against those of his schoolmates, while the master looked on and annexed the corpses of the slaughtered fowls to replenish his scanty table.

Other entertainments were regarded less leniently. When in 1725 the enterprising little Allan Ramsay opened a circulating library — the first ever formed in the kingdom — in the first floor of a "land" in the Luckenbooths, the arrival and circulation of profane books from London was regarded with opprobrium.

The magistrates sent some of their number to inspect the pernicious shelves; but, forewarned, the wily librarian kept out of sight the worst of his stock, and the civic detectives saw only an array of decorous works before them.

Dancing — 'a seductive temptation to sin'

In the dearth of public pleasures, the worldly energies of society found expression in concerts and dancing assemblies; and from 1710, when the first assembly was opened, it was at public balls that society met. The pulpits rang with denunciations of this seductive temptation to sin, lust, and worldliness; "promiscuous dancing" was condemned as an incentive to sensuality, and these rooms were pictured as nurseries of vice. But, in spite of all, society danced, and dancing-masters ran a flourishing business. These dancing teachers gave their own balls, in bigger rooms of a wynd. Tickets cost 2s. 6d. (12½p.); dancing began at five o'clock and went on till ten or eleven. There was also the assembly in the West Bow, in a flat facing the grim and haunted lodging of the wizard Major Weir; and in the narrow lane, from four o'clock, there was a crowd of sedan-chairs with their gaily attired occupants, the noisy mob pressing to witness the fine sight, the objurgations in safe Gaelic of competing chairmen, the clanking of swords of gentlemen in bright silken coats. Up the winding turnpike stair to a flat ladies ascended, holding up their hoops to gain difficult entrance by the narrow passage.

In this poor incommodious room, and after 1720 in the Assembly Close, off the High Street, the dancing revels took place, while the ministers uttered their solemn, ineffectual warning. Under the patronage of ladies of high degree, the minuet and the country dance went on with stiffness and with state in the low-roofed, hot, ill-ventilated room to the meagre music of a few fiddlers.

Each partner had been chosen by a gentleman before the ball, the selection being made at some private party, when all the fans were placed in a cocked hat, and the owner of the fan picked out became the partner for the night — each having a shrewd guess who was the fair owner of the fan he took. The tickets were then bought by the gentleman, who sometimes had one or two oranges stowed away in his coat pocket for the refreshment of his lady, who sucked them during pauses of conversation and intervals in the dance — a succulent process which she varied by presenting to her nose delicate pinches of snuff, which she extracted from the dainty snuff-box hanging by her side. The customary price for the ticket was two shillings and sixpence (12½p.), not defraying the modest expenses of tea and coffee which were consumed in the card-room, and the proceeds of the ball were devoted to charity — especially to the new Royal Infirmary, which was enlisting popular interest.

Days and nights in the taverns and coffee houses

There was another aspect of ancient Edinburgh society, which presents the fairer and more refined conditions of a life which had much that was coarse in manners and uncultivated in tone. Music was one of the favourite tastes of fashionable circles, especially when played by the distinguished amateurs of society. In a tavern — the "Cross Keys" — ladies and gentlemen from 1718 met in the afternoons to hear their musical friends, who gave "consorts", at which the best Italian sonatas were played on flute, hautbois, violoncello, and harpsichord. Artistic noblemen and lairds who had travelled to the melodious south brought the pieces which they (aided by professional musicians) performed to an enthusiastic throng of beauties, who went into raptures as my Lords Colvil and Haddington sat down to the harpsichord or the 'cello. When these grew old, others took their place in seat and platform in St Cecilia's Hall in the dingy, dirty Cowgate. The songs of the country, too, were not neglected either at these public reunions or at tea-parties in the flats, to which the sedan-chairs bore their be-hooped, be-powdered occupants, where they partook of fare as simple as the airs they sang.

Drinking and tavern-frequenting form, in contrast to this artistic aspect of society, a curious characteristic of Scottish town life. In Edinburgh, accommodation being extremely limited in the dwelling-houses, there were no rooms in which to transact business with clients or to give entertainments to friends. Men were therefore obliged to resort to the tavern or coffee-house, where the charges were moderate and the rooms were convenient. In these hostelries in the narrow wynds off the High Street tradesmen made their settlements, and drank with their customers to "wet" a bargain. Silversmiths located in Parliament Close made arrangements in John's Coffee-House to supply the present of silver spoons ordered by a bridegroom for his bride, and drank on the occasion a cup of ale at his customer's cost. There again he met his customer to hand over the spoons just arrived from London — for his own stock was small — and then they drank at his own expense, as the bill was being paid. In Paxton's dingy tavern magistrates met to "splice the rope" — the convivial term for the entertainment at which they arranged the details for a hanging. In the tavern advocates met with the writers, when, according to etiquette, the member of the bar had the choice of the morning beverage — usually sherry in a mutchkin stoup — before the case was discussed; and, if the case was won, client, lawyer, and advocate fraternised once more to celebrate the triumph. So essential was this convivial process that the first and last items in a lawyer's account were the charges of the tavern bill. In the simpler, ruder days, about 1730, Lord Kames says that when the French wine was put down in a tin pint vessel a single drinking-glass served a company for an entire evening, and the first persons who called for a fresh glass with each new pint were considered too luxurious.

In taverns the Lord Provost had his guests to dinner and to supper, where they could drink deeper and longer than in his private house. During the annual meetings of the General Assembly of the Church they were swarming with ministers and elders, who, after long parting, quaffed with a preliminary grace, their friend's good health at meeting. It might happen there was a dispute as to the right of patronage between two lairds or lords; and the rival claimants for the right to appoint the parish minister each sought to win over to his side the ministers before whom his case came to be tried in the Assembly. They regaled those whose votes they wanted freely at breakfast, at dinner, or any other time, in a tavern, while some interested lady of quality also invited them to tea; and after being bribed by her grace and her blandishments, the worthy country ministers would descend the turnpike stair loud in praise of her "leddyship", and proceed to vote convincedly in favour of my lord. No function was so great that it could not be celebrated in those dark rooms in unsalubrious wynds; no functionary was so lofty in rank and position that he could not reside in those unpretentious places of entertainment. In Clerihew's or Fortune's Inn the Lord High Commissioner held his receptions, and gave his dinner-parties for the members of the General Assembly and the magnates of the town, and thence the procession in limp dignity walked with a bevy of ladies behind to the ecclesiastical senate in St Giles'.

Often, however, the transaction of business was more the excuse than the reason for attendance in taverns. It was a convivial age, and it was a drinking society. When St Giles' bells played out half-past eleven in the morning each citizen went to get a gill of ale, which was known as his "meridian", although before breakfast he had paid a similar visit, and in the course of the day he went not seldom with his customers to drink over their bargains. It is not surprising that he was unable to transact his business at times, however highly respectable he might be. In the evening citizens were back at their familiar haunt to spend the evening with congenial friends over a simple fare, with ale or claret, till the town guard beat the ten o'clock drum, warning all decent burghers to withdraw soberly to bed. In the early part of the century the civic law prohibiting all persons from being in taverns and change-houses, cellars, etc, after ten o'clock at night, under penalties at the discretion of the magistrates, according to the degree of their contumacy, was a rule prudently obeyed, and as the tattoo on the drum echoed up the High Street and down the Canongate the inns and cellars disgorged their convivial contents, and in varied stages of inebriety the citizens departed stumbling on the uneven causeway, the younger loiterers repeating with unsteady voice the refrain of the last toping song. In the dark streets came the various companies, young clerks and roistering bucks, and, not infrequently, old merchants and unsober judges, who also made the wynds vocal with their bacchanalian strains.

Her Edinburgh bibles outraged society

Besides a social life not always refined and dignified, there gradually appeared signs of literary interest, though they were not very clear or brilliant. In the early part of the century Edinburgh — which implies all Scotland — was well-nigh destitute of literature. The strife — political, social, and religious — had been too long and loud for the voices of poets to be heard; the turmoil of parties was too keen for quiet culture to flourish; the condition of society was too poor, and the taste of the country too rough, for letters to be cultivated. In bygone generations the press had been busy, and printing had been excellent; but when the century began, except a few pamphlets, and inconsiderable works on law, or politics and controversy, nothing was printed except poor editions of favourite devotional works in execrable type. The widow of Anderson, the late king's master printer, claimed inheritance of his patent, giving a practical monopoly of printing Bibles, catechisms, school-books, editions of notable divinity and Bibles, with power to prevent the importation of editions from abroad. Vigorously she prosecuted publishers in Edinburgh, Glasgow, and far-off Aberdeen; although it was vehemently protested that her folios of Poole's *Annotations* and Flavel's works — the great authorities of ministers — were "voluminous blotches"; that her Bibles were scandals — bad type, bad spelling, full of blasphemous blunders, shameful mangling of Holy Writ, fearful printing, where italic and roman were confusedly blended in the same word, and lines where all words ran into each other to form stupendous hieroglyphics. No wonder; for she kept no corrector of the press. The importunate widow only gave way when law and patience could endure her exactions no longer. The best printers of the time were Jacobites; but in many a cellar there were printers, working creaking old machines brought from Holland, to whom Whigs and Presbyterians sent their manuscripts, which came forth in mean pamphlets, with paper, type and shape miserable to behold.

But, after all, there was little literature to suffer from these troubles. Dr Archibald Pitcairn, scholar and physician and wit, got his verses and Latin elegies printed on sheets, and handed them to his friends, and a few writers of little importance had a furtive publicity. But the first literature worthy to survive came from the little wig-maker's shop at the sign of the Mercury in the High Street — satires and songs that were printed on broadsides, and sold for a penny. Since 1711 Allan Ramsay had been writing, making wigs, if not "barberising" customers in his night-cap, albeit he boasted his descent from the honourable house of Dalhousie. In 1721 his collected poems were published; in 1725 his *Gentle Shepherd* appeared. He had given up his wigs and his curling-tongs, and transferred the books he had begun to sell to the flat in the Luckenbooths, over which he placed his new sign — the heads of Ben Jonson and Drummond of Hawthornden. He filled his shelves with books for sale, conspicuous among them his edition of the *Gentle Shepherd* from Ruddiman's press in "Turkey clad"; and he got from London a supply of works to lend out on his forming the first circulating library in the country. His shop was the resort of all that were literary and genial; his presence the merriest and vainest at the Easy Club, where "men of parts" recited their own verses and heard mild essays, and men of good fellowship sang jovially, and drank copiously, till long past "the drum." No figure was more familiar in the streets than the poet's, then "a dapper, neat little man of five feet four"; in mellower years, a squat form with big paunch, fair round wig above a humorous countenance, expressive of great self-satisfaction. Where could Mr John Gay, when visiting her eccentric Grace the Duchess of Queensberry, find more congenial talk than in the brother poet's shop? There the English bard — remembered as "a pleasant little man in a tye-wig", paunchy like his friend — exchanged news of the London world of letters for explanation of obscure words in the ex-wigmaker's Scots, and gazed from the window with amusement at the gay, busy throng that promenaded the High Street from one to two o'clock each day.

Successful as Ramsay was with his poems, which brought fame and guineas to his till, there was scanty encouragement for letters — no patrons worth an author's obsequious dedication, few book-lovers to subscribe for even the smallest edition of a work, no public that cared to buy. Wisely, in 1725, James Thomson went to England with his poem on *Winter* in his pocket. Eleven years later Smollett set off to London by pack-horse with his surgeon's lancets and his *Regicide* in his bag. There, too, Malloch had gone to seek scope for his talents in English society, and had changed his name to Mallet to suit the English ears. Meanwhile, booksellers in obscure booths in Parliament Close dealt mainly in divinity — Durham on *The Song of Solomon, The Balm of Gilead,* Rutherford's *Letters,* historical tracates, vehement pamphlets of scholars and divines, and poorly printed classics imported for schools from Holland. The news of the day was sparingly conveyed in puny sheets twice a week, the chief being the *Edinburgh Evening Courant* (first issued in 1718), in the interest of the Whigs, and the *Caledonian Mercury* (which appeared in 1720), favoured by the Tories. But it was difficult to extract any interest from those newspapers that gave no news, containing a London letter giving meagre tidings of what had happened long before, or never happened at all, intelligence of a vessel arrived with timber and tallow yesterday at Leith, and advertisements of half a dozen "roups" next week.

Port and dancing in the oyster cellars

Ladies did not hesitate at times to follow the jocund ways of the stronger sex. In company with gentlemen, in wild spirits they would go into the oyster cellars in "laigh" shops, dirty, squalid rooms below the street, and by the flickering light of guttering tallow candles regale themselves on raw oysters and porter, and dance together in the sordid cell, which echoed with their laughter and the clatter of their high-heeled shoes. Then escorted home, they allowed their partners to adjourn once more, and with punch and brandy toast their "flames" with hiccoughing chivalry. "The misses are the most rotten part of the society", wrote in disapproval the most proper and stately Lady Elliot of Minto.

But in spite of all such vagaries, the social life in some of its moral aspects stands out conspicuously pure compared with that of England. Scandals of married life were few, and brought down social disgrace when they did occur, and the character of womanhood in the middle and higher orders was singularly honourable. Speech was certainly not refined, and was often strangely lacking in delicacy; but the conduct was strict, though the tongue seemed free.

Later in the century the ten o'clock signal might sound, but the topers sat on, magistrates being the most habitual violators of their own laws, and men drank not merely "from the gill-bell to the drum", but long after. Clubs there were of all kinds — for wits and cits, for solid traders and spendthrift youths, for judges and clerks, for men of law, men of letters, and men of leisure — clubs bearing strange names, whose meaning is lost and fine humour has evaporated; but though the company varied, the purpose was ever the same. It must be said that the expenditure of time was the chief expense, for the favourite dishes were cheap — minced collops, rizared haddocks or tripe, a fluke or roasted skate and onions, for which the sum of sixpence was charged. The "Spendthrift Club" enjoyed itself immensely at fourpence half-penny a head.

Literary genius of Edinburgh

But of real literature, save the poems of Ramsay, there were still few signs; till in 1738, there appeared in London a *Treatise of Human Nature* by David Hume, then twenty-five years old. It fell, as the author cheerfully confesses, "still-born from the press"; which did not discourage him from publishing, within a few years, those philosophical essays which slowly established his name in literature and his place in sceptical philosophy, creating a panic fright in orthodox circles, which was borne with placidity by the simple-souled and good-humoured philosopher — verily, the "mildest-mannered man that ever scuttled" a creed.

After the middle of the century there was a wider awakening of intellectual life in Edinburgh, and in Scotland generally. Hume was busy with his *History of England,* which began to appear in 1754; his friend Home was writing his tragedy of *Douglas* in his manse at Athelstaneford; Dr Robertson was engaged with his *History of Scotland*, which was to make him famous in the winter of 1759. Adam Ferguson, Hugh Blair, Adam Smith, and others, were soon to make Edinburgh a literary centre and literature a matter of fashion to gentlemen. At that time the effort was not to write Scots, but to learn to write English. Home, Reid, Robertson strove indefatigably to clear their pages of every provincial idiom, and every Scotsman anxiously consulted English friends for guidance and correction. They fairly succeeded, but not without pains, for Dr Beattie owned that "we who live in Scotland are obliged to study English for books like a dead language which we can understand but cannot speak. Our style smells of the lamp and we are slaves of the language, and are continually afraid of committing gross blunders." Accordingly the author of the *Minstrel* had pored over Addison, Swift, and Lord Lyttleton to learn to write this foreign tongue — labours which met their reward, when he became the idol of blue-stockings in London, and fashionable circles mistook an "elegant writer" for a profound philosopher. Naturally these authors published their works in London, but naturally they chose countrymen to publish them, for eminent Scots booksellers abounded in the capital — Millar, Strahan, and Murray.

Intellectual activity was spreading in all circles. The Select Society, founded by the versatile and energetic Allan Ramsay, the portrait-painter, changed in 1755 to the Society for Encouraging Art, Science, and Industry. Noblemen, lairds, judges, ministers, advocates, engaged in these meetings — not unconnected with suppers and claret — for promoting husbandry, linen trade, and the fostering of art — which it did by offering prizes for drawings that never won them. At the Bar there were men of wit and forensic ability who afterwards made themselves conspicuous on the bench or even famous in the senate; there were men of science and philosophy who redeemed the University from the obscurity under which it had lain for generations; and ecclesiastics of distinction who by their good-breeding rebutted the wholesale charges of uncouthness against the clergy, and by their tolerance were to relieve them from the indiscriminate taint of fanaticism. These men were well-known figures in the crowded streets of Edinburgh. As one looked, about 1771, down from the lofty windows in the High Street, opposite the place where the old Market Cross had stood near St Giles', and where the citizens and townsfolk most did congregate, there were more men of note to be seen in an afternoon than could have before been seen in a century.

Creech's bookshop, in the premises at the Luckenbooths, below old Allan Ramsay's flat, was where gathered daily the quidnuncs of the town, to see the newest books from London, and to hear of the newest arrivals from the country, or to chat with the worthy bibliophile as he stood on the steps.

Church loses its grip

At the close of the century the Church's grip on people was loosening considerably. "Men of fashion" were deserting the pews in their droves.

The theatre also had greatly lost its stigma, and the clergy had ceased to ban it. In fact, when Mrs Siddons came to act, ministers went in such numbers that the General Assembly, then sitting, was half-deserted by its members; and pious sober-minded citizens were induced to go, though with fear and trembling, to the perilous playhouse, for the tragedy queen had made it almost respectable. A staid old lawyer was persuaded to visit the theatre for the first time in his life to see the great actess in *Venice Preserved.* When the catastrophe came he turned to his daughter and asked if this was a comedy or a tragedy? "Bless me! papa, a tragedy to be sure!" "So I thought", remarked the worthy man; "for I am beginning to feel a commotion."

Other tastes had changed, though not always for the better. Mr William Creech, who in his bookshop in the Luckenbooths met with wits, citizens, and literati, and from his windows, which looked down the long High Street, watched a tide of humanity as ever-flowing if not so varied as that which rejoiced Dr Johnson in Fleet Street, saw and heard much to bewail about 1780-1790, in a degenerate age — cock-pits increasing and church attendance diminishing, people that were worldly and ministers that were lax in their visitations; but at any rate he does own that immoderate drinking and "pushing the bottle" was in 1790 going out of fashion with educated people, "pressing" was not so common, and every one was allowed at table to do as he pleased in filling or drinking his glass.

Policing the city

While society was making its own rules for the morals and manners of fashionable circles, a decrepit police was trying to maintain good order in the city, and to suppress crime. It might be supposed that in a town abounding in intricate wynds, dingy closes, and dark stairs, and with a large class steeped in poverty, lawlessness and robbery would be common. But, on the contrary, there seems to have prevailed a remarkable immunity from crime. The fact that every one knew everybody, the intimate contact of high and low, rich and poor, may have served as a sort of social detectivism, and made theft rare, by the comparative ease with which culprits could be watched.

The charge of order and the preservation of the lieges was committed to a small and effete band of city guards, consisting of 120 men all told — very few of whom were kept on duty, the others acting more usefully as porters or scavengers. A long low building that blocked and disfigured the High Street, opposite the Tolbooth, formed the headquarters of these old Highlanders, most of them discharged soldiers, who guarded the lives and adorned the processions of the city, armed with preposterous Lochaber axes. They were sources of mirth rather than of safety, these much provoked worthies, nicknamed the "town rottens" (or "rats"), who never could catch an offender, and poured forth their futile Gaelic oaths at urchins who sorely mocked them. Outside the shed in which they were stationed was a wooden horse, which drunkards were made ignominiously to bestride; and under the shed was a cellar, to which disturbers of the civic peace were consigned at night.

Such a system of police, which might have served in a little town, had become ludicrous long before it was superseded by more stalwart men to look after a city with a wider radius and large population. Yet in spite of all, throughout the century — as, indeed, through all the country — there were very few serious offences. Housebreaking and robbery are said to have been extremely rare, and with complete sense of security people seldom thought of locking their doors at night. Except in such seasons as when the notorious Deacon Brodie and his confederates perpetrated their burglaries (1783-1787), there was little danger felt. In the Tolbooth prison, among its few inmates were more debtors than criminals; and years passed by without any execution, though robbery was a capital offence. Probably the chief, most venial, and most prevailing offence was drunkenness.

The Edinburgh Revolution

By 1770 there were signs setting in of the approaching transformation of Edinburgh — in the city and society. It was full time, for the crowd of inhabitants was now denser, and the streets and wynds were as malodorous as ever. One night arm-in-arm Boswell and Dr Johnson marched slowly up the High Street, inhaling the "evening effluvia." Then the great man grumbled into the ear of his friend, "Sir, I can smell you in the dark!" The town, which had remained within its ancient bounds and walls for 250 years, was becoming too circumscribed for its population, which filled the streets that had grown in height instead of length; spaces behind the Canongate and High Street, once occupied by pleasant gardens, had long been built over by wynds and courts, and no more room was left for its increasing inhabitants to build on. About 1760 there had been erected squares of "self-contained" houses south of the town, to which some richer families resorted; and yet, though only a few minutes' walk from their business and their friends, Brown Square and George Square were considered terribly out of the way, so that gentlemen required to take refreshment in the tavern before the journey. In 1772 the North Bridge was finished, and access to a new district became easier, while old merchants spoke with astonishment about the enormous rents of £30 or £40 which ambitious rivals were paying for shops beside the "Brig." Plans by that time had been formed for streets on the other side of the "Nor' Loch" (the lake or swamp now the Princes Street Gardens); but slow progress was made till 1780, when new streets were springing up, and houses in Princes Street, George Street, and Queen Street were advancing westward. From the old flats descended in gradual exodus persons of position and quality, who, instead of a modest rental of £15 or £20, were able now, through advancing wealth and larger incomes, to pay £100 for mansions which contrasted strangely with the mean and dirty abodes from which they emerged. They left those dwellings where there had been little cleanliness or comfort, where fetid air brought sickness and death to young lives, where infectious diseases passed like wildfire through the inmates of a crowded common stair, bringing havoc to many a household.

Town and town-life underwent a revolution, and many a quaintly pleasant and picturesque feature of Scottish society soon became a mere memory. Fortunately, the old taverns lost their "genteel" company, and gentlemen met temperately at home in their spacious dining-rooms, instead of in miserable cellars, over their mutchkin and glass. The sedan-chairs were becoming worn out, like the chairmen who had carried in them so many fair occupants, with towering powdered headdresses, to the dance, and for 6d an hour had shaken their burdens over the causeway, and up closes where no carriage could enter. These were being discarded for hackney coaches that drove swiftly along handsome though unfinished streets; but for many a year some ladies of the olden type were still borne along to their tea-parties in the venerable chairs of their grand-mothers. Other changes came — some that were not grateful. The delightful old simplicity of manners, the unceremonious friendliness, the genial gatherings around the tea-table, where the company discussed their "fifty friends within five hundred yards"; the familiar intercourse and sympathy between rich and poor, formed by proximity in the same turnpike stair; the quaint old dowager ladies of rank and poverty, who, on "small genteel incomes", and with one maid-servant, kept up a tiny establishment and gave slender entertainments in a fourth flat, — all these passed away for ever.

By the close of the century these "lands", in multitudinous closes, were becoming deserted by the upper classes. Although some clung on tenaciously to their patrimonial tenements, the bulk of quality and fashion had gone to reside on the other side of the swampy North Loch, quitting for ever the old haunts where so long a teeming friendly population of gentle and simple had dwelt, leaving for ever ancient flats associated with ages of dirt and dignity, of smells and social mirth. The old rooms received new occupants — pawnbrokers lived where lords of session had dwelt; washerwomen cleaned clothes in chambers where fine ladies had worn them; mechanics, with their squalling brats, occupied apartments whose decorated mantelpieces and painted ceilings told of departed greatness — rooms where in bygone days the gayest of the town had met, when they were scenes of all that had been brightest and merriest of olden life.

With the New Town of Edinburgh began a new social existence in Scotland.

EDINBURGH LIFE IN THE NINETEENTH CENTURY

By
William Gilbert

LANG SYNE PUBLISHERS LTD.

INTRODUCTION

The year is 1800 and Edinburgh is not a happy place. Many folk are living on the starvation line because food is scarce and expensive. The hungry take part in frequent riots plundering shops of what little goods are available.

Beggars infest the streets. Cases of robberies and muggings are shooting through the roof. Unfortunately civic authorities, saddled with an inadequate system of policing, are essentially impotent to act.

But as the decades of the period covered in these pages — 1800 to 1900 — start to roll by a new city emerges which is eager to take up the challenges presented by wonderful inventions and the benefits of universal education and voting systems.

The pages of the diary record how oil lamps give way to gas lighting. Later we witness the arrival of electricity. With the 1840s comes the birth of railway fever. Lines spread out from "Modern Athens" in all directions and everyone is keen to sample the new mode of transport.

The years tick by and Auld Reekie's population multiplies by the thousand. The boundaries are expanding too as houses and factories and schools and stores are built. Portobello has risen from a lump of wasteland to become one of Scotland's most popular resorts. Some of our greatest institutions and most famous landmarks are born .... and this diary unfolds the events as they happen.

In many cases we meet horror and violence. A great fire leaves 400 families homeless. Burke and Hare, bodysnatchers most foul, are exposed. Thousands fall victim of the killer disease cholera. Public hangings are a social occasion to be followed by a lively discussion in the pub once the executioner has completed his duty.

1800

FAMINE IN THE CITY. - The war, arising out of the grim events of the French Revolution, had an effect upon Edinburgh and the country at large which, fortunately, the present generation, engrossed in the thrilling events of the campaign in South Africa, have no experience of. The war against the Boer Republics may have raised the income-tax to 1s per £1, but it has not interfered in the slightest degree with the food-supply of the country. Both in Edinburgh and Glasgow in 1800 food was scarce and dear. Meal, which formed a large part of the dietary of the common people, was dear, and 'meal-mobs' were not uncommon in both cities. Many essays appear in the local periodicals of the day, written with the view of explaining the causes of the distress — one opinion, put forth with great authority, being that the misery and famine were caused by the extravagant number of horses kept on the land. The fact was that there had been a poor oat-harvest all over Europe as well as in Britain, and that the countries from which oats were generally imported had barely enough to serve their own necessities. The crisis, however, was sufficiently grave to cause the Lord Provost and Magistrates of Edinburgh to turn their attention to it. They had conferences with the corn-merchants and dealers in wheat, and as a result of these meetings they, in conjunction with the Sheriff, issued an address, dated April 25, 1800, in which they assured the people that, while meal was scarce, there was a sufficiency of other kinds of grain, and they therefore earnestly recommended the inhabitants to consume as little oatmeal as possible, and to make wheat and barley-meal their chief article of food. They go on to say that wheat-meal mixed with one-half of barley-meal makes most excellent food, either in the shape of cakes or porridge, and that a peck of meal, half wheat, half barley, which every family can mix for themselves, can at present be retailed for about 2s 4d per peck. In this address we find further, that the Magistrates and Sheriff call in the most earnest manner on every person, high and low, 'to be as economical of all kinds of meal and flour as possible, and in particular, that all persons keeping horses only for carriages or riding, should on no account feed them on oats, but give them only barley bruised, which is much more nutritious than when given whole.' This paternal advice is signed by James Stirling, Provost, and James Clerk, Sheriff-Depute.

This method of quieting the people had evidently not been effective, for three days after the same gentlemen issued an official proclamation, recounting their belief in the virtues of wheat and barley-meal, holding out a hope that prices would soon be reduced, but warning the inhabitants to avoid any tumultuous assembly for the future, 'as the magistrates will take the most vigorous measures for repressing any tumultuous or riotous meetings of the populace which may hereafter occur, being satisfied that they proceed from the wicked views of bad and designing people.'

Fortunately the harvest of 1800 was fairly abundant and early, and the people of Edinburgh, under the advice and admonition of their rulers, seem to have behaved in an orderly way until it was gathered in. Possibly they found that to eat wheat-meal, or even that mixed with barley-meal, was not so great a hardship as they seem at first to have considered it. On a certain Tuesday in August it is chronicled that there were in the market no less than 307 bolls of meal, which is said to be 'the greatest quantity there has been there this year at one time.'

The famine had a redeeming side, inasmuch as it called forth the sympathies of the richer inhabitants for their poorer brethren, and several voluntary subscriptions were raised to ameliorate the lot of those in distress. The distress, however, was so great that the Town Council got from Parliament 'The

Edinburgh Poor Bill', for the better relief of the poor of the city of Edinburgh, under which they took powers to raise a sum of £10,000 by assessment to be dispensed by way of relief. It is also put on record that the respectable families of the city had entered into resolutions to discontinue the use of fresh butter until it comes to one shilling per pound. This 'boycott' was evidently put into effect, for it is grimly added, 'in consequence of which the butter-carriers remained in the market this day with their butter unsold.'

1801

THE EDINBURGH VOLUNTEERS. — In the last years of the eighteenth century, and the early years of the nineteenth century, Edinburgh had a splendid corps of Volunteers, over 3000 strong, which was brought into existence for home defence against the threatened invasion of Napoleon Buonaparte. Such a body of men, recruited for the most part from the best of the citizens, drilling and exercising, and being reviewed, naturally for the time was an important element in the life of the city. They were known as the Royal Edinburgh Volunteer Brigade, and comprised both artillery and infantry. Frequent references are made to the volunteers in the literature of the day, especially in the year 1801, when rumours of invasion were rife and the country was on the alert to repel attack. The volunteers were exercised on Bruntsfield Links, or Leith Links, in tactics for repelling an enemy landing on our shores; there were reviews by His Excellency General Vyse, commanding at that time in Scotland, who always said very complimentary things about the corps; and on September 1, 1801, the Lord-Advocate Hope, as Lieutenant-Colonel commanding the 1st Regiment of the Royal Edinburgh Volunteers, made a tender of the service of that corps to the Government in a spirited and patriotic letter. He recalled the fact that when the French fleet appeared in Bantry Bay in 1796, the Edinburgh Volunteers made an offer to take garrison duty at the Castle in case it were found necessary to withdraw the regiment doing duty there.

LEITH HARBOUR. — A sure sign of the increasing commercial activity and prosperity of the city was the resolution on the part of the authorities of Edinburgh, who owned the Port of Leith, to provide better harbour accommodation for the shipping frequenting it. In 1799 the magistrates obtained an Act authorising them to borrow £160,000 to execute part of a range of docks designed by Mr John Rennie, C.E.; but it was not until May 1801 that the foundation-stone of the eastern wet docks was laid.

EARTHQUAKE. — It is recorded that in 1801 the city experienced a smart shock of earthquake. It occurred on the 7th September, and was distinctly felt at Edinburgh, Leith, and the neighbourhood. So extensive a shock had not been felt in Scotland since the earthquake at Lisbon. It ran across the island from Greenock to Leith, the centre of it being at Crieff or Comrie. What is pointed out as a remarkable circumstance in connection with the shock was that, while it was sensibly felt in the New Town, it did not seem to have been felt in the Old Town or to the south of that. No damage was done at the moment by the earthquake, though it got the credit of having caused the fall of a barn to the west of the city a few days later, which killed two shearers who were sleeping in it, and the sinking of a tenement in Paterson's Close, which was thereupon condemned by the Dean of Guild Court.

BEGGARS — The magistrates issued an order that all beggars in the city should be committed to Bridewell, but to prevent unnecessary hardship the House of Industry was instituted under the patronage of the Queen, for the reception of those men, women, and children who are willing to work.

DRAINING OF THE MEADOWS. — The Town Council resolve to have the Meadows drained, with the view of giving employment to the industrious poor who at this season are without work.

LEGAL AND PARLIAMENTARY — The Right Hon. Robert Dundas of Arniston, having been appointed Lord Chief Baron of the Court of Exchequer, vacated his seat in Parliament for the county of Midlothian, which he had held for eleven years, and Robert Dundas of Melville Castle was appointed in his place.

ILLUMINATION OF THE CITY. — There was great joy in the city on the ratification of the proclamation of peace between this country and France. The Volunteers paraded in the Meadows (13th October) and marching to Princes Street, and facing the Castle, fired a *feu-de-joie*, while the big guns aloft thundered out a royal salute. There was an immense crowd of spectators. In the evening the bells were set a-ringing, and the city was brilliantly illuminated. A number of transparencies which had for some time been in preparation were exhibited, with appropriate emblems, inscriptions, etc. This was followed by the shipment from Leith of 208 French and 24 Dutch prisoners, who had been confined in Edinburgh.

1802

EXTENSION OF THE ROYALTY. — The Provost and Council present a petition for leave to bring in a Bill for embodying the City Police and extending the royalty over the lands of Bellevue, for enlarging York Place, and for other purposes of public improvement and ornament.

PROPOSED CANAL. — March 11, there was a full meeting held in the Merchants' Hall, to consider the plans of the intended canal from the West Country to Edinburgh. Different opinions prevailed with regard to the line of ground through which the canal was to be brought. The Hon. Henry Erskine made a motion, which was unanimously agreed to, that different subscriptions should be opened for the various plans proposed, and the plan to be decided by the majority of the subscriptions.

KING'S BIRTHDAY. — June 4th, the sixty-fifth birthday of the King was celebrated in Edinburgh with the usual demonstrations of joy. There was a salute from the guns of the Castle, and from the battery at Leith, and in the afternoon the magistrates gave a grand collation in the Parliament Hall to a number of noblemen and gentlemen. There was also an assembly in the evening. The chronicler of the day reports that 'it is beyond the recollection of the oldest citizen that they ever observed at any former period such general happiness unsullied with riot or outrage', 'and it affords a pleasing prospect that in time coming our city will no longer be reproached with those dangerous and filthy demonstrations of tumultuous joy which endangered its inhabitants and disgraced its police.'

OYSTERS. — September 13th, the Magistrates made a regulation in the fish-market, by which the best oysters are to be sold at 2s (10p) per 130 from the 1st December to the 1st March, and from the 1st March to the 1st December, 1s. 6d (7½p) per 130.

REORGANISING THE POLICE. — Robberies and street offences having become common, a numerous and respectable meeting of the inhabitants was held on 29th November, at which resolutions were agreed to, declaring that the present system of police by means of the town guard is defective, and not adapted to the increased extent and population of the city, and recommending the obtaining of an Act of Parliament for better watching of the city and suburbs of Edinburgh, and for the raising by assessment the expense of the new police establishment.

1803.

— EDINBURGH AND GLASGOW MAILS. —
March 2nd, a new arrangement has been made by the Postmaster General, in consequence of which the mail from the city to Glasgow is to be conveyed in the mail cart, the driver of which is to be armed with a cutlass and pistols. This mode will afford a greater degree of security than formerly.

DEFENCE ASSOCIATIONS. — The French having again broken the peace, meetings were held for the defence of the city and neighbourhood, and volunteer companies were again embodied, including a Highland corps 500 strong. In respect that the members of the Presbytery of Edinburgh could not give personal service, they offered a bounty of £2. 2s. to the first hundred able-bodied men who, between the 1st August and 15th September, should enlist in any branch of His Majesty's service. The 1st regiment of Royal Edinburgh Volunteers again embodied received their colours from the Lord Provost, Mr Neil Macvicar, at a parade at the Market Cross, 22nd September. This regiment, clothed in scarlet, was reviewed a month later on Bruntsfield Links and, with their artillery corps, mustered 1104 men. Two companies of Loyal Edinburgh Spearmen, or pikemen, were also embodied. How real the sense of danger of invasion was may be gathered from the fact that Edinburgh was provisioned as if for a siege, and that each family that could afford it was invited to lay in at least ten days' provisions for their own use.

BUILDINGS. — Notwithstanding the expensive war in which the country was engaged, it is recorded that the improvements in the city of Edinburgh and Leith continued to go on with rapidity. This year a great part of the Luckenbooths was pulled down, the High Street widened where they stood, and the beautiful old Cathedral of St Giles opened to public view. Considerable progress has been made in the new harbour at Leith; the elegant bank for the Bank of Scotland is nearly finished; and a great number of beautiful houses and shops have been built on the north and south sides of the city.

1805

A CAUSE CELEBRE. — Mr John Leslie having been elected Professor of Mathematics in the University of Edinburgh, the Presbytery objected to the appointment on the ground of certain opinions expressed by him in an article contained in a publication on 'Heat', certain members holding that it invalidated the argument for the existence of the Deity. At the same time, the Presbytery called on the Senatus to see that certain Acts of Parliament were carried out which enjoined that every member of the professorial body, in all the faculties, should sign the Confession of Faith. The case excited an immense amount of interest in the city; it was debated at great length in the Presbytery and Synod, and in the General Assembly, to which it was carried on appeal. The supreme court of the Church, however, threw out the reference, and the matter thus ended.

THE NEW POLICE ACT. — This Act, passed April 1805, came into force the following May. It for the first time divided the city and suburbs into six wards, one of which included Portobello, and constituted a body of General Police Commissioners for administrative purposes. Police, cleaning and lighting, and a variety of other duties were given to the Commissioners. The streets were named, the houses numbered, a survey made of them to fix the rents for assessment purposes, and a Judge of Police appointed, the first holder of the office being Mr John Tait, who was, with much speaking, solemnly inducted, on the 15th July, by the Lord Provost and Magistrates, the Sheriff of the county, the Member for the city, and the Commissioners of Police. The Court of Police was opened the same day at the Office of Police, Riddell's Close, Lawnmarket, and six inspectors were elected, one for each of the six wards into which the city had been divided. It was a great occasion for the city, the bringing into operation of the new Police Act placing its watching and lighting and cleaning on a footing there had never been before.

THE OLD CITY GUARD. — One of the effects of the new police *regime* was the practical abolition of the Old City Guard, which had existed since 1696. One company, however, consisting of one lieutenant, two sergeants, two corporals, two drummers, and thirty men, were retained, their duties being to attend on His Majesty's Commissioner, on the Magistrates and Supreme Courts, and to act in general in support of the police if ordered to do so by the superintendent.

TRAFALGAR. — The great naval victory of Lord Nelson was celebrated by rejoicings in Edinburgh and by the illumination of the city. The illuminations, we are informed, were mixed with many patriotic remembrances of the gallant hero of the Nile. A subscription list was opened for the relief of the relatives of those who fell at Trafalgar; a proposal was made to erect a monument in Edinburgh to Lord Nelson; and on the 5th December, which was the day appointed by His Majesty for a general thanksgiving to Almighty God for the brilliant successes of the British arms, many of the people who went to church wore mourning out of respect to Nelson's memory.

1806

NEW WET DOCK, LEITH. — May 20th, there was a procession of the Lord Provost, Magistrates, and Council, and a numerous company of ladies and gentlemen, at the opening of this dock. The Fifeshire packet and a smack called *The Buccleuch* were the first to enter the dock, with the civic dignitaries on board, amid discharges of artillery from the Fort at Leith and His Majesty's ships of war in the Roads. This dock, it is put on record, is the first of the kind in North Britain. It has been wholly executed within high-water mark, and the space occupied by it is five acres. Including, however, the ground at its sides and ends, on which it is proposed to construct graving-docks, building-slips, sheds, and warehouses, the area taken from the sea was fifteen acres.

LORD MELVILLE. — The trial, in the House of Peers, of Lord Melville on charges of high crimes and misdemeanours alleged to have been committed by him while Treasurer of the Navy, created great interest in Scotland. Malversation of public funds was a leading count in the indictment. His acquittal on the 12th June was received with general satisfaction in Edinburgh, the Town Council of which, and many other public bodies, voted him congratulations. The city would have been illuminated but for a dread that it would have led to a riot and the wrecking of the houses of some persons opposed to him.

THUNDERSTORM. — A memorable thunderstorm took place in Edinburgh on 9th August. The thunder and lightning continued without intermission from two in the afternoon till past eight o'clock in the evening. Great damage was done by the rain which accompanied it, all over the country.

BEGBIE'S MURDER. — William Begbie, porter to the British Linen Company's Bank, situated in Tweeddale's Close, High Street, while going through the entry from the street to the bank, carrying a bag containing bank-notes to the value of £4392, which he was bringing from an agency in Leith, was stabbed through the heart and robbed of the money. The weapon used was a common bread-knife with a wooden handle, which was found near the spot. There was a great hue and cry; a reward of 500 guineas was offered for information which would lead to the conviction of the murderer; but the assassin, despite every exertion made to track him down, was never discovered. Part of the money stolen, being in £20 notes which the robber had been afraid to pass, was afterwards found in the hole of an old wall at the foot of Broughton Street.

1807

THE EDINBURGH UNIVERSITY. — The building scheme of the University having been suspended for want of funds, it was seriously proposed that a lottery should be opened to provide money for its completion.

PROPOSED FORTH TUNNEL. — In this year a scheme was proposed for tunnelling under the Firth of Forth, so as to give a continuous land communication between the Lothians and Fife. A pamphlet was published by James Miller, M.D., and William Vazie, to prove its practicability. The point where it was proposed the tunnel should be was at Queensferry, where the Forth Bridge now stands.

PORTOBELLO. — New salt-water baths were this year erected at Portobello at a cost of £5000. The *Scots Magazine*, sketching the rise of Portobello, says: — 'It is within the remembrance of many persons yet living that the lands called Figgate, on which Portobello is now built, were a perfect waste covered almost entirely with whins or furze. As a proof of the sterility of these lands, the whole, amounting to seventy acres, were let not much above forty years ago for 200 merks Scots of yearly rent, a sum little exceeding £11 sterling. But in the year 1762 or 1763 these were sold by Lord Milton to Baron Mure for about £1500, and afterwards feued out by the latter to Mr Jameson at the rate of £3 per acre; and such has been the rise of value, that some parts of the same lands have been lately disposed of at a yearly feu-duty of £40 per annum for every acre.'

NEW TOWN CHURCHES. — An agitation was commenced for the purpose of having more churches provided for the New Town. It is stated that 'in the whole magnificent and widely extended New Town of Edinburgh and its vicinity, containing at least 14,000 or 15,000 inhabitants, there is at present only one public church of the established religion of Scotland for the whole inhabitants of the place.'

THE NELSON MONUMENT — On Wednesday, October 21, being the anniversary of the battle of Trafalgar, the foundation stone of Lord Nelson's monument was laid on the Calton Hill. In consequence of the inadequacy of the funds, an 'elegant design' by Mr Nasmyth had to be relinquished, and a less expensive one by Mr Burn, architect, adopted. It was originally proposed that a considerable space round the monument should be railed in and used as a burial-ground for the army and navy.

1808

MARMION. — *Marmion*, or *A Tale of Flodden Field*, by Walter Scott, was published and was received with great enthusiasm by the public.

THE COURT OF SESSION. — The great improvements in wealth and commercial industry having occasioned a vast increase in the number of litigations, and as since the era of the Union — that is, for more than a hundred years — no alterations had been made on the mode of administering justice, a Bill was introduced into Parliament 'touching the administration of justice in Scotland and appeals to the House of Lords.' After much discussion and amendment it was passed, and the Court was divided into two divisions.

1812

SANGUINARY NEW YEAR RIOTS. — The night of the 31st December 1811, and the early morning of the 1st January 1812, were disgraced by a series of riots, outrages, and robberies hitherto without example. After eleven o'clock at night the principal streets were taken possession of by bands of rough young men and boys from the lower parts of the town, armed with bludgeons, who assaulted, and for the time overcame the police, and knocked down and robbed of their money, watches, and hats many respectable inhabitants. Dugald Campbell, a policeman, and James Campbell, a clerk, died of the wounds received on the occasion, and two rewards of one hundred guineas each were offered for the discovery of the murderers. A number of youths were arrested, and three tried at the High Court on the 20th March, viz. Hugh M'Donald, Hugh M'Intosh, and Neil Sutherland, were convicted for being art and part in the murders and of robbery, and were executed on a gibbet and scaffold erected opposite the Stamp Office Close, High Street, where the policeman had been killed. The three youths were all under eighteen years of age. The execution, which created a tremendous sensation in the city, having been intended as a dreadful example to the disorderly apprentices and boys of the city for years to come, everything about it, including a procession from the Tolbooth to the scaffold, was studiously contrived to impart solemnity to the awful scene. Such a concourse of people as witnessed this execution had never, it is said, been seen before in the streets of Edinburgh.

REORGANISATION OF THE POLICE. — One of the effects of the riot was the reorganisation of the police establishment, and the closing of the Court presided over by Mr

Tait, Judge of Police, who had been appointed seven years previously. In that time 12,000 police cases had passed through his hands.

THE ASTRONOMICAL INSTITUTION. — This Institution for the prosecution of the study of astronomy was established, and by its exertions the Observatory on the Calton Hill was erected. The first President was Professor Playfair.

MEAL MOB. — In consequence of prevailing destitution among the poorer inhabitants of the city there was a meal mob riot on 18th August. Crowds assembled in the Cowgate and Grassmarket, seized the farmers' carts coming into the city, and attacked the shops of victual-dealers and bakers in Nicolson Street. The Magistrates ordered out the military, and quelled the tumult. The same evening they issued a proclamation enjoining all to avoid riotous proceedings, and assuring the inhabitants that they would do all in their power to relieve them from their present distress. A subscription was opened, and a considerable sum collected was dispensed by the elders of the different kirk-sessions.

1813

HIGH STREET FIRE. — By a fire which occurred on the 14th February 'the Bishop's Land on the north side of High Street was destroyed.'

ROMAN CATHOLIC CHAPEL. — The Roman Catholic Chapel, Broughton Street — a handsome Gothic edifice built by subscription at a cost of £8000 — opened.

BEGGING. — A society for the suppression of begging instituted. The city seemed at this time infested with beggars, and it was proposed to strictly apply the Vagrancy Acts and assist at the same time the deserving poor. A total of 622 cases of professional beggars was dealt with in the first year.

PRICE OF PROVISIONS. — There was great distress among the poor consequent on the high price of provisions. The following shows the rise that had taken place on the prices of the necessaries of life between 1760 and 1813:—

	1760	1813
Wheat per quarter, .	£2 0 0	£6 10 0
Malt " .	1 8 0	4 12 0
Flour per bushel, .	0 5 10	1 2 6
Bread per quarter loaf, .	0 0 8	0 1 6½
Pork per lb., .	0 0 4	0 1 0
Butcher meat per lb., .	0 0 4	0 1 0
Cheese " .	0 0 4	0 1 1
Butter " .	0 0 6	0 1 10
Sugar " .	0 0 8	0 1 1
Pair of shoes, .	0 5 0	0 12 0
Soap and candles per lb., .	0 0 6	0 1 1½

FREEDOM OF THE CITY TO WALTER SCOTT — On the 22nd December the Lord Provost, Magistrates, and Council voted the freedom of the city to Mr Walter Scott as a mark of their esteem for his literary talents. On the same occasion the freedom of the city was presented to the Earl of Dalhousie, who had distinguished himself at the battles of Vittoria and of the Pyrenees, and to Sir Thomas Graham.

NEW INSURANCE COMPANY. — The Scottish Widows' Fund and Life Assurance Society instituted.

ILLUMINATION OF THE CITY. — On the occasion of the entry of the Allied Armies into Paris the city was splendidly illuminated, 15th April. Edinburgh is said never before to have presented so brilliant a spectacle. A feature of the decorations was a grand triumphal arch over South Bridge Street.

REGENT BRIDGE AND CALTON JAIL. — An Act of Parliament was obtained for building a bridge over the Low Calton and for opening up a new entrance to the city from the east; also for erecting and maintaining a new jail on the Calton Hill. The Lord Provost and Magistrates, one of the contributing bodies, were authorised to raise £12,000 towards the expense of the building.

LEITH AND NEWHAVEN. — On the 11th April, with procession and ceremony, the foundation stone was laid of the new church for the parish of North Leith. On the 15th of the same month the foundation stone of the new harbour at Newhaven was laid.

SPECULATIVE SOCIETY'S JUBILEE. — The jubilee of this Society was celebrated the 17th December. Twenty-eight toasts were on the programme, and it is related that several others were drunk. Principal Baird, who presided, left the chair at nine o'clock, and nominated as his successor Mr Walter Scott; and we are told that 'the gay conviviality of mood' (of the author of *Waverley*) 'and his inexhaustible fund of wit and pleasantry contributed greatly towards the hilarity and harmony of the remainder of the evening.' The concluding toast given from the chair was, 'May the next half century impart as much pleasure to the new members as the last one has done to the old.'

1815

AN EXECUTION IN THE SUBURBS. — Two criminals, Kelly and O'Neill, were executed 25th January on the Morningside Road, at the Braid Burn, near the spot where they had committed a highway robbery.

NEWS OF WATERLOO. — The important intelligence of the glorious and decisive victory of Waterloo on the 18th June was forwarded by express to Edinburgh by Sir John Marjoribanks, the Lord Provost, then in London, and reached the city on Saturday, 24th June, about eleven o'clock. The news was received by all ranks with great satisfaction, and the thanks of the Council were next day voted to the Lord Provost for so promptly affording to his fellow-citizens the accounts of this splendid event.

THE EDINBURGH UNIVERSITY BUILDINGS. — After the new buildings for the Edinburgh University were commenced, it was found that the money collected, though considerable, was not sufficient for the erection of the large and elegant structure which had been designed. The work was accordingly stopped until this year, when the House of Commons voted a grant of £10,000 towards the completion of the University, and agreed to continue the same annually for seven years.

RIOT IN THE HIGH STREET. — There was a riot in the High Street, 5th June. The police were pelted with stones and driven into the police-office, and a sergeant of police, George Hone, died of the injuries he received on the occasion.

NEW EPISCOPAL CHURCHES. — St John's Episcopal Chapel, Princes Street, designed by Mr William Burn for Bishop Sandford's congregation, Rose Street, was commenced. St Paul's Episcopal Chapel, York Place, designed by Mr Archibald Elliot for the congregation worshipping in the Cowgate Episcopal Chapel, was also projected this year.

REGENT BRIDGE AND NEW JAIL. — The foundation stones of the Regent Bridge and the new Calton Jail were laid on the 19th September. There was an imposing masonic and civic procession from the High Church to the site of these buildings, it being recorded that it was 'the most brilliant procession which ever adorned the annals of Masonry.' Two thousand Masons were present on the occasion, and though the weather was unfavourable, there was an immense assemblance of spectators.

1816

NEW JURY COURT — On the 22nd January a new Jury Court for the trial of civil cases with the assistance of a jury was opened. The Lord Chief Commissioner, as the head of this Court was named, was the Right Hon. William Adam, one of the Barons of Exchequer, and the other Commissioners were Lord Meadowbank and Lord Pitmilly. The first case tried was at the instance of Mr (afterwards Sir) Henry Raeburn.

THE EDINBURGH RACES. — This year, for the first time, the Caledonian Hunt and Edinburgh Races were run at Musselburgh, instead of on Leith Sands, where they had been held in the past. The change was very advantageous. The races lasted a week, and on the Friday there were about 50,000 spectators. At the Theatre for the week there was a special engagement of 'the celebrated tragic actor, Mr Kean, from Drury Lane Theatre.'

RUSSIAN PRINCE IN EDINBURGH. — On the 16th December the Grand Duke Nicholas of Russia, brother of the Czar Alexander, paid a visit to the city, and was received with due ceremony. In the course of his stay he was presented with the freedom of the city, and was entertained by the Lord Provost to a banquet in his house in Charlotte Square. His Royal Highness contributed £100 to a subscription then afloat for the relief of the working classes of the city suffering from the depression of trade.

1817

NEW COUNTY BUILDINGS. — These buildings, on the west side of Parliament Square, were erected, at an expense of £15,000 from designs by Mr Archibald Elliot. The plan was taken from a celebrated Greek model — the Temple of Erechtheus on the Acropolis of Athens.

THE 'SCOTSMAN' NEWSPAPER. — The prospectus of the *Scotsman* newspaper was issued 30th November 1816, and the first copy of the paper was published on the 25th January 1817. Its size was four pages, each 14½ inches by 10 inches, and its price 10d. This included a Government stamp of 4d per copy.

DISTRESS IN THE CITY. — The committee for the relief of workmen out of employment had over sixteen hundred men on their list. These workmen were employed in making roads on the Calton Hill, along the front of the Salisbury Crags, sloping the banks of the Nor' Loch, and levelling parts of Bruntsfield Links. About £10,000 was expended in road-making in this way in various parts of the city, the subscriptions including one of £1000 from the Prince Regent.

GAS LIGHT COMPANY. — The Edinburgh Gas Light Company formed with 800 shares of £25 each. Lord Provost Arbuthnot was the first Governor, and Sir John Marjoribanks of Lees, Bart, M.P., Deputy Governor.

HIGH STREET IMPROVEMENTS. — The old jail, the only part of the old Luckenbooths remaining, was begun to be demolished, 18th September. The criminal prisoners were removed to the new Calton Jail, and the debtors, twelve in number, were liberated, their debts having been generously paid by a subscription among the inhabitants. The old jail was erected in 1561. It was originally designed for the accommodation of Parliament and the Courts of Justice, and also for the confinement of debtors and criminals. After 1640 it was used solely as a jail.

BURGH REFORM. — The Edinburgh Merchant Company began to agitate for Burgh Reform. At a meeting held on 17th November resolutions declaring for the introduction into Scottish burghs of 'a more rational and liberal system of town polity' were, on the motion of Mr Adam Black, carried by a large majority.

THE OLD TOWN GUARD. — This ancient body was disbanded in November, according to the provisions of a recent Police Act. The Edinburgh Town Guard was originally raised in the year 1648, and consisted of 60 men and their officers. In 1682 it was raised to 108 men. For many years there were three companies of one captain, one sergeant, one corporal, one drummer, and twenty-five privates. They wore a quaint uniform, and were armed with Lochaber axes.

1818

DISCOVERY OF THE REGALIA OF SCOTLAND. An idea prevailed in Scotland that the ancient regalia had been removed to England. Commissioners appointed by the Prince Regent made an examination of the Crown Room at the Castle, 5th February. Nothing was in the room but a large oblong oaken chest. This they directed to be forced open, and it was found to contain the crown, sceptre, and sword of state of Scotland in a state of perfect and splendid preservation. The

Lord Treasurer's rod of office of silver gilt was also there. So soon as the existence of these venerable and precious relics was ascertained the Royal Standard was hoisted and the soldiers cheered, a salute which was heartily echoed from the Castle Hill.

THE UNION CANAL. — The first spadeful of this extensive work, to connect Edinburgh and Glasgow by water, was dug at Fountainbridge, 3rd March, by Mr Dowie of Appin, chairman of the Company, in presence of a large assemblage. The cost was estimated at £235,167.

SHOCKING AFFAIR AT AN EXECUTION. — Robert Johnstone, twenty-three years of age, was executed, December 30, for highway robbery. Being the first execution after the removal of the old jail, a scaffold was erected, the gibbet of which rested on the wall of St Giles' Cathedral. Owing to the imperfect construction of the scaffold, when the drop fell the culprit rested on his tiptoes. The mob stoned the magistrates and police off the platform, cut down the victim, restored him to his senses, and carried him off. In the High Street the mob were attacked by the police, and Johnstone was recaptured. In the meantime the Provost had brought a company of soldiers, with loaded rifles, from the Castle, who surrounded the scaffold, to which the wretched man was again dragged and hung.

1819

WATER COMPANY INCORPORATED. — At a meeting held on the 12th February it was resolved to form a joint-stock company for the supply of Edinburgh with water.

THE NATIONAL MONUMENT. — On Wednesday, 3rd March, a meeting of noblemen and gentlemen was held to promote a National Monument to commemorate the 'unparalleled victories' of the late wars. The Duke of Atholl presided. It was agreed that such a memorial should be erected in the capital — that it should comprehend a church, ornamented in such a manner as to perpetuate the memory of the great naval and military achievements.

THE FINE ARTS — An institution, for the encouragement of the Fine Arts in Scotland was founded, and held its first exhibition of loan pictures in the studio of Mr Raeburn, York Place.

1820

DEATH OF KING GEORGE III AND PROCLAMATION OF HIS SUCCESSOR. — The old King died 29th January 1820, in the eighty-second year of his age and sixtieth of his reign. On the 3rd February George IV was proclaimed at the Cross of Edinburgh with great ceremony. The procession also went to the Castle Esplanade, the Palace of Holyrood, and the pier and shore of Leith, and at all these places the King was likewise proclaimed.

PARLIAMENTARY ELECTION. — At the general election, consequent on the death of the King, the Hon. William Dundas was re-elected by the Magistrates and Council member for the city. The proceedings were noteworthy from the fact that three of the Deacons of the Trades, Sawers, Morham, and Paterson — for the first time, probably, in the history of such transactions — declined to vote, as a protest against Mr Dundas's opposition to Reform.

SIR WALTER SCOTT. — The citizens read with great

satisfaction the announcement in the *Gazette* of 1st April that the King had made Mr Walter Scott of Abbotsford a baronet. Sir Walter was the first baronet created after the King's accession.

THE ORIGINAL SECEDERS. — On Friday, 8th September, the Associate Synod (the Burgher) and the General Associate Synod (the Anti-burgher) reunited. The gathering was held in the Bristo Street meeting-house, where it is recorded the separation took place seventy-three years before.

QUEEN CAROLINE. — The bill of pains and penalties against the consort of George IV having been thrown out of the Lords, November 19th, the people who sided with the Queen partially illuminated the city, against the wishes of the magistrates. The mob broke the windows of the non-illuminators; and damage was done to the extent, it was said, of £10,000, for which the city was afterwards assessed. The military from Piershill and the Castle were called out.

STAGE-COACHES. — The number of stage-coaches to London now number fourteen weekly.

1821

POPULATION OF EDINBURGH AND LEITH. — By the census returns of last year it was found that the population of Edinburgh and Leith was 138,235, Leith being about 26,000.

THE NOR' LOCH. — That part of it which lies to the west of the Mound was enclosed, drained, and planted with trees, and shrubs and walks formed in it.

THE WATERLOO HOTEL. — This hotel at Regent's Bridge was built by subscription at a cost of £30,000.

STEAM-PACKETS. — This year steam-packets were first introduced between Leith and London. The first, called *The Mountaineer,* was of 104 feet keel and of 40 horse-power, and was guaranteed to do the journey in sixty hours. Another steamer, of 400 tons and of 100 horse-power, called *The City of Edinburgh,* was the largest steam vessel built up to that time. It had beds for one hundred people, and cost £20,000.

THE EDINBURGH SCHOOL OF ARTS. — This association was established by a number of gentlemen friendly to the improvement of the Arts as applied to trade and manufacture. Its object was to enable industrious tradesmen to become acquainted with the principles of mechanics, chemistry, and such other branches of science as are of practical application to their several trades.

THE MELVILLE MONUMENT. — Saturday, 28th April, being the anniversary of the late Lord Viscount Melville, the foundation of the monument erected to his memory in the centre of St Andrew's Square by the Royal Navy and Marines of the United Kingdom, was laid by Admiral Sir David Milne, K.C.B., and Admiral Otway, Commander-in-Chief. The design of the column was chiefly copied from Trajan's Pillar at Rome. Pedestal and pillar are 136 feet 4 inches high, and the statue on the top is 14 feet additional.

1822

PRINCES STREET LIGHTED WITH GAS. — On the 10th January Princes Street was lighted with gas for the first time. Seventy-nine oil lamps were displaced by fifty-three gas lanterns.

A NOTABLE DUEL. — James Stuart of Dunearn was tried in the High Court for killing in a duel, on the 26th February, Sir Alexander Boswell of Auchinleck. The latter had lampooned Mr Stuart in a Glasgow paper called *The Sentinel.* The trial, which excited an unprecedented interest among all classes, resulted in the jury bringing in a verdict of not guilty.

THE EDINBURGH AND GLASGOW UNION CANAL. — This great undertaking, begun in 1818, was opened in May this year at an expense of nearly £400,000. It is thirty-one and a half miles in length.

THE REGISTER HOUSE. — This elegant Grecian edifice, planned by Robert Adam, was finished this year. It has a front of 200 feet, and a depth of 120 feet.

1824

BOTANIC GARDENS. — The Royal Botanical Garden, Leith Walk, having been found inconvenient, a new garden was acquired at Inverleith Row of eleven and a half Scots acres. It was opened in May.

OIL-GAS WORKS. — On May 24th the foundation-stone of an oil-gas work was laid at Tanfield by Sir Walter Scott, who was chairman of the company.

MONUMENT TO MR PITT. — The Pitt Club of Scotland on March 27th resolved to set aside £3000 of their funds towards erecting a monument to the memory of this great statesman.

GREAT FIRE. — About one o'clock of the morning of Thursday, 24th June, fire broke out in the back premises of a spirit-dealer at the head of the Royal Bank Close, High Street, and before it was extinguished it destroyed five houses of six

OLD NEWHAVEN

THE "TWA BRIGS", CRAMOND

PICARDY VILLAGE AND THE FORTH BEYOND

OLD RESTALRIG

THE CROSS OF EDINBURGH where men of genius and lesser mortals met to discuss affairs of the moment

THE OLD TOWN FROM PRINCES STREET

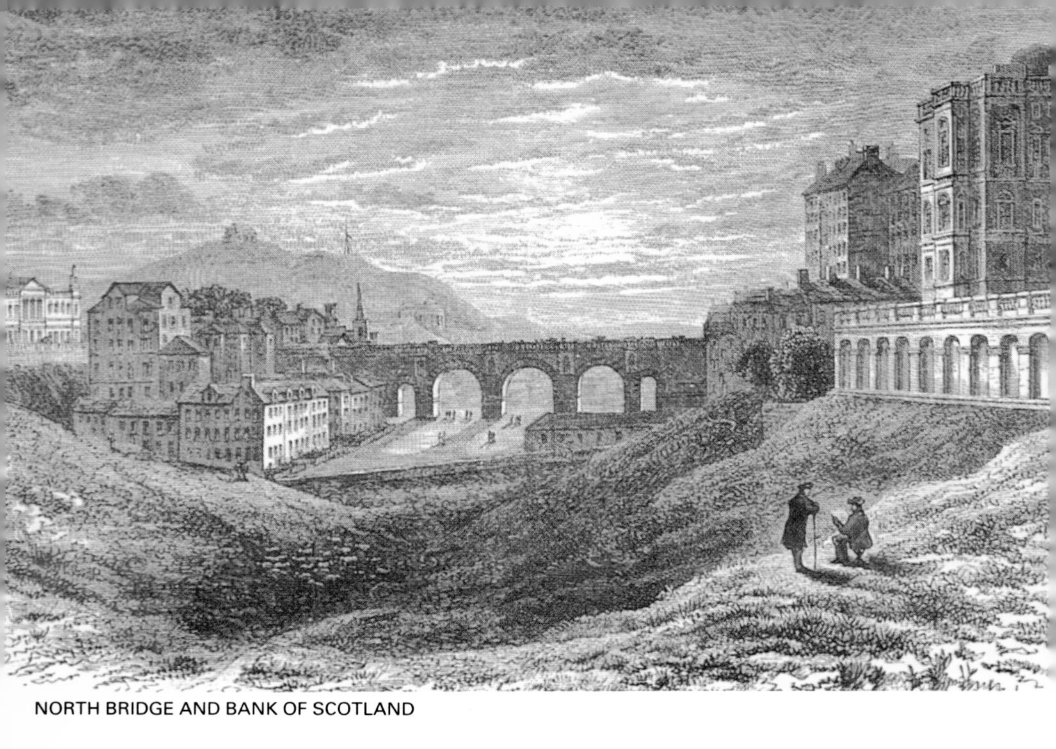

NORTH BRIDGE AND BANK OF SCOTLAND

GEORGE IV BRIDGE

stories high, comprising the tenements over the piazza leading into Parliament Square, one house in the Square, and the one in Royal Bank Close in which it had originated. A town's officer named Chalmers was so scorched in attempting to rescue some valuable papers that he died. The property on the same site was burned down in a great fire which occurred in 1700.

WATT INSTITUTION. — In memory of James Watt, the celebrated engineer, it was resolved to erect a memorial building to house the School of Arts, and to call it 'The Watt Institution.'

ARTISTS' DINNER. — At a dinner of artists held in the British Hotel, Queen Street, in commemoration of the distinguished honour conferred on the Fine Arts by the King on his visit to Scotland, Alexander Nasmyth was in the chair, and David Wilkie, R.A. (afterwards Sir David), was present as a guest.

EDINBURGH MUSIC FESTIVAL. — The third music festival was commenced on the 25th October. The morning performances were in the Parliament House, and the evening in the theatre. Three guineas were charged for a set of six tickets. The receipts were £4940. 4s. 10d., and the expenses £4397. 18s. 11d., leaving for distribution among the charities of the city £542. 5s. 11d. This decrease in the surplus, as compared with that of the two former festivals, was attributed to the 'high demands of the principal singers.'

GREAT CONFLAGRATION IN THE HIGH STREET. — The most disastrous fire recorded in the history of the city broke out on Monday night, the 15th November, about ten o'clock, in a large seven-storey house at the head of the Old Assembly Close, and, with the exception of one tenement left standing opposite the Cross, the whole buildings on the south side of the High Street, from the head of the Old Assembly Close round to the Exchequer buildings in Parliament Square, were destroyed, together with much of the property running backward to the Cowgate. The fire burned fiercely the whole night, the old houses, full of dry wooden panelling, affording abundant food for the flames, which only began to abate about nine o'clock on the following morning. While the conflagration was raging great showers of sparks and burning embers fell upon the street and adjoining buildings, some of which were fired in that way. A tenement, in which the *Courant* newspaper office was situated, was totally destroyed. To the west of this the conflagration was arrested by the fact that the tenement overtopped the others by a story. On Tuesday forenoon, when all danger seemed to be past, the steeple of the Tron Church was discovered to be on fire. Some burning embers had been carried to the balustrade, and had been fanned into a flame by the wind, which, though it had been calm all night, was now blowing a gale. The steeple was of wood cased in lead, and blazed furiously. The firemen had to fly for their lives, for the molten lead poured down the sides of the structure, and rendered it impossible to approach it with safety. The heat was so great that a large bell weighing two tons, which had been hung in 1673, was fused. The steeple burned for three-quarters of an hour, and then fell with a crash. By great exertions the firemen managed to save the church. The same evening, fire broke out again in a tenement on the south side of Parliament Square, with its back overlooking the Cowgate. It was an immense pile, eleven storeys in height, and it burned with irresistible fury. The flames spread to the east side of the Square, and all that was left standing by the June fire was then involved in the general destruction. The value of the property destroyed by these conflagrations was estimated at £200,000, nearly four hundred families werre rendered for the time homeless, and eight individuals were either killed on the spot by the falling of ruins or died from their injuries. Along the front of the High Street there were destroyed four lands of six storeys each; towards Cowgate by Con's Close, two wooden lands; in the Old Assembly Close, four lands of six or seven storeys; six smaller tenements in Borthwick's Close; and four lands of from six to nine stories in the Old Fishmarket Close. Along the front of Parliament Square four double lands, of from seven to eleven storeys in height, were destroyed. The dangerous walls left standing of the burned houses were brought down on the following Saturday by means of a chain cable and apparatus worked by a body of H.M. seamen, and partly by mining with gunpowder. Many of the homeless people found temporary shelter in Queensberry House, at that time belonging to the Government, and a subscription was opened for them which soon amounted to £7000. Twenty-two fire-engines belonging to the Insurance Companies were in operation at the fire, and the military from the Castle, Piershill, and Leith Fort, and the Yeomanry, were called out to keep order or to assist the firemen. The whole city was filled with consternation at the calamitous event, and little business was transacted in the week in which it occurred. One effect of the conflagration was the purchase by the city of several engines of the newest type, and the organisation of a fire brigade.

PATRONAGE ABOLITION ASSOCIATION. — A Society was founded in Edinburgh, 24th December, for the purpose of improving, with a view to its ultimate abolition, Church Patronage in Scotland.

1825.

MORE FIRES. — A disastrous fire on the 22nd February again threw the city into alarm. It occurred in a house six storeys high at the head of Blackfriars Wynd, known as Lady Lovat's house, which, with the upper flats of one adjoining fronting the High Street, was destroyed. On the 17th of April there was also a disastrous fire in Milne's Court, Lawnmarket, which ruined a tenement.

JOHN WATSON'S CHARITY. — The foundation-stone of John Watson's Hospital, near Bell's Mills, was laid 4th July. Mr Burn was the architect. The money had been left under the Trust of the Keepers and Commissioners of the Signet in 1781.

ROYAL HIGH SCHOOL. — The foundation-stone of the new Royal High School was laid with masonic honours, 28th July, in presence of a great crowd of spectators. The boys marched in the procession. The building was estimated to cost £17,000.

1826

WEST INDIAN SLAVERY. — A large public meeting was held on the 1st February, the Earl of Rosebery in the chair, to petition for the mitigation and ultimate abolition of Slavery in the West Indies.

SALISBURY CRAGS. — The Earl of Haddington, Keeper of the King's Park, having for many years quarried for road metal at Salisbury Crags — which operations threatened their destruction — his right was challenged in the law-courts. The objectionable practice was stopped on a hint being given to the Earl by King George IV. In 1843 the Earl's rights in the Park were bought up by the Government for £30,000, and the Park placed under the management of the Woods and Forests.

ROYAL INSTITUTION. — The buildings of the Royal Institution, Mound, opened 13th February.

1828

BURKE AND HARE MURDERS. — The city and country generally were thrown into a state of alarm by the discovery of the Burke and Hare murders. These wretched criminals decoyed such people as they thought would not be missed, chiefly into a house in West Port, smothered them, and sold their bodies for dissecting purposes to one of the surgeons of the town, Dr Knox. The trial of Burke and Mary McDougal, his paramour, on the charge of murder, was begun in the High Court, 24th December. Hare and his woman were admitted as King's evidence. The woman got off, but Burke was found guilty and sentenced to be hung 28th January.

THE BEGINNING OF TEMPERANCE SOCIETIES. —

Mr Dunlop, Greenock, delivered an address, October 27, in Clyde Street Hall, on National Intemperance, his object being to form a temperance society upon the model of those in America.

AN EDITORIAL DUEL. — A duel took place at Ravelston between Mr Maclaren, editor of the *Scotsman*, and Mr James Browne, editor of the *Caledonian Mercury*, who in the first place had had a wordy warfare in the columns of these papers. Pistols were used, but after an exchange of shots, which did neither of the combatants harm, the seconds declared that the matter should not be carried further.

1830

THEATRICAL FUND DINNER. — At a Theatrical Fund dinner in aid of decayed Scottish theatrical artists, held 29th January, £300 was raised for the fund.

1832

CHOLERA MORBUS. — This pestilence, known as Asiatic cholera, made its first appearance in the city January 27. Some thousands succumbed to it in the course of the year. Thursday, February 9, was observed as a local day of humiliation and prayer in connection with its ravages, and there was a national day of prayer on the 22nd March.

NEW MAGAZINES. — *Chambers's Journal* and *Tait's Edinburgh Magazine* were commenced this year.

THE REFORM BILL. — The great event of the year was the passing of the Reform Bill. There were several monster processions of the Trades and meetings in support of it, and on the 10th August there was a 'jubilee' procession to celebrate the triumph of reform, in which 15,000 people took part. So great was the interest in the Bill that one Sunday from 12,000 to 15,000 people assembled on the Calton Hill to await the arrival of the express from London with the latest news of it. The hustings were erected at the Cross on the 17th December, when for the first time the candidates for the two seats given to Edinburgh by the Reform Act were publicly nominated. The Whigs proposed Lord Advocate Jeffrey and the Right Hon. James Abercromby, and the Tories Mr Forbes Hunter Blair. The poll stood — the Lord Advocate, 4036; Abercromby, 3843; Blair, 1519.

DEATH OF SIR WALTER SCOTT. — The city was greatly moved by the announcement, on the 21st September, of the death of Sir Walter Scott. On the 5th of October, at an influential meeting held in the Assembly Rooms, it was resolved to raise a monument to his memory. The Duke of Buccleuch presided, and the speakers included Lord Rosebery, Lord Advocate Jeffrey, Professor Wilson, and Lord Meadowbank.

1833

REPORTING THE TOWN COUNCIL PROCEEDINGS. — Reporters were first admitted to the Edinburgh Town Council meetings, 30th January.

EDINBURGH VOLUNTARY CHURCH ASSOCIATION. — This association, with the object of severing the connection of Church and State, was established at a meeting held 29th January in the Rev. Dr Brown's Church, Broughton Place.

ANNUITY TAX. — An agitation was commenced against the annuity or stipend tax, January 21. Mr W Tait, bookseller, having refused to pay this tax, was the first to be sent to prison. On his release from the Calton he was escorted home by Trades with a triumphal procession.

PITT STATUE. — This statue, by Mr Chantrey, was erected in George Street.

THE DEAN BRIDGE. — This handsome bridge, designed by Mr Telford, erected almost at the sole expense of Mr John Learmouth, Lord Provost, was built by John Gibb and Son, contractors, Aberdeen. It was intended to open up the Dean estate to feuing. The roadway is 120 feet above the Water of Leith.

ORPHAN HOSPITAL. — This building, begun in 1831, was finished, October this year, at a cost of £16,000.

BURGH REFORM. — The Burgh Reform Act having passed through Parliament, Edinburgh for municipal purposes was divided into five wards, each returning six members, with the exception of the Fourth ward, which had seven. There were fifty candidates for thirty-one seats, and not a single Tory was returned, the Council consisting of twenty-four or twenty-five Whigs and seven or eight Radicals. Among the men returned at this first popular election were Adam Black, Duncan M'Laren, and William Chambers. The first Lord Provost elected by a popular franchise was the Right Hon. James Spittal, of Justice Hall. The bailies, four in number, were Robert Thomson, J F Macfarlane, Thos. Sawers, and James Donaldson; and Adam Black was Treasurer. The Dean of Guild and the Convener of Trades were also members of the Council.

1834

STATUE OF THE EARL OF HOPETOUN. — An equestrian statue in bronze of the Earl of Hopetoun was erected at the east end of St Andrew Square.

1835

STATUE OF CHARLES II. — On May 9th the equestrian statue of Charles II, which had been taken down for repairs, was re-erected in Parliament Square.

THE HIGH STREET. — The High Street was lowered, which caused a flight of steps to be placed at the entrance to St Giles'. During the operations the workmen found the foundations of an old jail, the celebrated 'Heart of Midlothian.'

THE WEST BOW. — Many old houses were pulled down to make way for new improvements, among others that of the reputed wizard, Weir of Kirkton, who with his sister perished at the stake in 1670.

PHILOSOPHICAL SOCIETY. — The Philosophical Society

of Edinburgh was instituted for the furtherance of Science and Art.

LIBBERTON'S WYND. — The arch of this wynd, the former place of execution, was removed.

1836

1836. SAVINGS BANK. — The National Savings Bank established 5th February.

NEW CHURCHES. — On July 11th, the foundation-stone of a new church was laid in Young Street; the ancient church at Restalrig was restored; new churches were opened at Greenside, Dean, and St Leonard's.

CHALMERS HOSPITAL. — George Chalmers, plumber, Canongate, died on March 10th, and bequeathed £30,000 to the Dean and Faculty of Advocates to erect and endow a new infirmary or hospital.

SOLAR ECLIPSE. — An annular eclipse of the sun took place during the afternoon of Sunday, May 15th. The interest excited by the phenomenon was tremendous, the afternoon service being postponed in most of the churches. Venus was seen shining brightly.

FETTES ENDOWMENT. — Sir William Fettes, Bart, of Comely Bank, died May 27th, and left the bulk of his fortune to form an endowment for the erection of an hospital for the maintenance and education of children whose parents had fallen into adverse circumstances.

EDINBURGH, LEITH, AND NEWHAVEN RAILWAY. — In August an Act was obtained for making this railway, which began at the east end of Princes Street Gardens, passed underground to the foot of Scotland Street, and thence to Trinity in a straight line.

GREAT FIRE. — A fire broke out during the night of December 27, which consumed a large woodyard and twelve or thirteen high tenement houses in Greenside Street, Greenside Row, and Nottingham Place.

1837

QUEEN VICTORIA. — Proclamation of Queen Victoria as Sovereign of these realms was made at the Cross, the Castle, and Holyrood House, on June 24th.

PRINTING. — On July 12th, the fourth centenary of the invention of Printing was celebrated at Edinburgh by over eleven hundred people. Thomas Campbell, author of *The Pleasures of Hope,* presided.

1838

THE SCOTT MONUMENT. — The committee accepted, 28th March, the beautiful Gothic design of George Meikle Kemp for the monument to Sir Walter Scott in Princes Street, and at the same time gave the commission for the statue to Mr John Steell, R.S.A. The foundation-stone of the monument was laid with masonic honours, 15th August 1840, by Sir James Forrest of Comiston, Lord Provost of the city, and Master Mason of Scotland. The gifted architect was unfortunately accidentally drowned, 6th March 1844, in the canal, and the monument was completed under the superintendence of his brother-in-law, Mr Bonnar, R.S.A. On 17th August 1846 the monument was formally inaugurated by the Lord Provost of the day, Mr Adam Black. It is 200 feet 6 inches high from the level of Princes Street, and is ascended from within by 287 steps.

CORONATION OF THE QUEEN. — The Coronation of Queen Victoria was celebrated on June 28th by a public banquet. In the evening there was a display of fireworks, and a bonfire on Arthur Seat.

HISTORICAL STONE. — Stone discovered in Cowgate, September 17th, on which the mutilated remains of Argyll, Montrose, and other distinguished persons were fixed, and displayed on the city gate at the South Back of the Canongate, nearly two centuries previous.

THE CITY DEBT. — According to a report presented by Mr Adam Black when he was Treasurer of the city, Edinburgh so long ago as 1653 had great difficulty in paying its debts, and it had continued in difficulty from that time until 1835. In 1658 the city debt was £54,761; in 1693, £73,000; in 1798, £160,000; in 1817, £212,000; and in 1833, £410,000. In these days large sums of money were expended in building city churches, on the care of the poor, and on the development of Leith Docks. Affairs had become very embarrassed in the Thirties, sequestrations were threatened, and the matter was taken up in earnest by Mr Adam Black, and by his successor in the treasurership, Mr Duncan M'Laren, the latter of whom carried through the City Agreement Act, 1838. By that Act the creditors of the city were secured to the full amount of their debts by receiving bonds of annuity of 3 per cent on the amounts due. The city's monetary interest in Leith Docks was represented by the payment annually by the Leith Docks Commission of £7680, which was distributed in certain proportions among the common good, the University, High School, and city ministers. The amount outstanding on the passing of the Agreement Act was £385,000. This arrangement continued until the Corporation Stock Act, 1894, was passed, Mr George M'Crae being treasurer. Under this Act the Leith Dock Commission paid to the Corporation £189,333 in commutation of annuities which at that date were £5680; and this and money raised by the issue of stock was applied to the extinction of the old debt, which between 1838 asnd 1894 had by redemptions been reduced to £298,633. In lieu of what was before obtained from the Leith Dock money the city now pays direct out of the common good to the University and High School annuities amounting to £2500. By the Stock Act and the extinction of the old debt the city regained complete control over its own revenues and expenditure. At the 1st August 1894 the capital sum at the credit of the commmon good of the city was £459,326.

1839

CHURCHES. — The foundation-stone of Buccleuch Parish Church was laid on April 3rd; on April 17th the foundation-stone of St John's Parish Church, Victoria Street, was laid; the church at Greenside was opened October 6th.

1840

PENNY POST. — The uniform rate of 1d. per letter of half-an-ounce weight was commenced on January 10th.

NEW BRIDGE. — New bridge erected over the Water of Leith at Canonmills.

1841

'THE TRUE SCOTSMAN.' — A paper of this name,

which had had a struggling existence in the city for two years, came to an end on March 27th.

THE CORN LAWS. — A petition from Edinburgh for the repeal of the Corn Laws received 27,000 signatures.

CHARLES DICKENS. — The eminent novelist was entertained to a public dinner in the city

HERIOT TRUST FREE SCHOOLS. — Free schools in connection with the Heriot Trust, to accommodate 2000 poor children, were founded.

BIRTH OF PRINCE OF WALES. — On the news reaching the city of the birth of the Prince of Wales, 9th November, the bells were rung, guns were fired from the Castle, an address was voted by the Corporation to the Queen, and a subscription was opened for the benefit of the poor in place of the usual illumination. The Lord Provost gave a banquet in the Parliament House to representative citizens on the 15th.

CENSUS. — The population of Edinburgh, according to the census of 1841, was 133,692: 58,642 males, and 75.050 females. Leith had 26.020.

1842

NORTH BRITISH RAILWAY. — On the 9th February the prospectus of the North British Railway Company was issued, the capital being £500,000. The object stated to be to connect the rich agricultural districts of Haddington and Berwick with Edinburgh, and to form a link in the chain of connection with England.

EDINBURGH AND GLASGOW RAILWAY. — This railway was opened on the 18th February. The line took three years to complete, and cost a million and a quarter sterling. Trains carrying the directors and their friends came from Glasgow to Edinburgh in the forenoon, and in the afternoon trains with fifty-two carriages went from Edinburgh to Glasgow, where there was a great banquet. The Edinburgh people were delayed three and a half hours in their return journey by some miscreant cutting the Cowlairs rope.

SUNDAY TRAINS. — When the various railways were first opened, great battles took place on the subject of Sunday Trains. On the Edinburgh and Glasgow Railway a morning and evening train were run each way on Sundays; but the Sabbath Observance members on the Board became strong enough to stop them for several years. The subject formed a constant source of discussion at the Town Council and Presbytery meetings, and at the meetings of the General Assembly.

THE QUEEN'S VISIT. — The Queen and Prince Albert paid their first visit to Scotland. Her Majesty arrived in the Forth on Wednesday, 31st August, and landing at Granton next morning before eight o'clock, drove through the city to Dalkeith Palace.

1845

BURNING OF GREYFRIARS' CHURCH. — On Sunday morning, 19th January, the Old Greyfriars' Church was totally destroyed, and the New Greyfriars' Church, which is under the same roof, was greatly damaged by fire. The rebuilding of these edifices formed a subject of much controversy in the Town Council and Edinburgh Presbytery.

SANITARY IMPROVEMENT. — At a public meeting of the inhabitants on the 20th March, it was resolved to form an association to promote the sanitary improvement of the city and the improvement of the condition of the working classes.

1846

GREAT GALE. — A furious gale, accompanied by great destruction of property and loss of life, was experienced in the Edinburgh district 4th March.

NORTH BRITISH RAILWAY. — This railway from Edinburgh to Berwick was opened 18th June. Two trains, one with twelve carriages and four engines, and the other with twenty-six carriages and five engines, took a company of seven hundred people over the line, and there was a lunch at Dunbar. By the completion of the line from Berwick to Newcastle, in September of the same year, London and Edinburgh were united by railway.

HERIOT'S HOSPITAL. — In consequence of an insurrection in the hospital, fifty-two boys were dismissed.

1847

EDINBURGH AND BATHGATE RAILWAY — The first sod of this railway was cut 9th April 1847.

RAGGED SCHOOLS. — An influential meeting was held, April 8th, for the purpose of instituting ragged or reformatory schools for poor children. The one with which Dr Guthrie's name is connected was first established, but a controversy afterwards arose as to the admission of Catholic children, and this led to the formation of the United Industrial School, to which children of all denominations could be admitted.

THE UNITED PRESBYTERIAN CHURCH. — The United Associate Synod and the Synod of the Relief Church amalgamated at a meeting held in Canonmills Hall, May 13th, and formed the United Presbyterian Church.

1850

FREE HIGH CHURCH. — This church was opened on 3rd February.

WEST END EXTENSION. — The extension of the New Town at the north end of Dean Bridge was begun in April. Clarendon Crescent, Cambridge Terrace, Eton Terrace, Oxford Terrace, and Leuchars Terrace were constructed.

ROYAL VISITORS. — On August 29th, Queen Victoria and Prince Albert arrived at Holyrood and passed two days at the Palace *en route* for Balmoral. On August 30th, His Royal Highness Prince Albert laid the foundation-stone of the National Gallery of Art at the Mound. Returning from Balmoral on October 10th, the Queen and Prince Albert spent one night at Holyrood. The town was illuminated.

1851

INAUGURATION OF DONALDSON'S HOSPITAL. The inauguration of Donaldson's Hospital took place, in presence of a large and representative company, on February 3rd.

NEW SLAUGHTER-HOUSE. — The Lord Provost, Magistrates, and Council assembled at Heriot's Hospital on 31st March, where they robed, and afterwards marched in procession to Fountainbridge, where the ceremony of laying the foundation-stone of the slaughter-house took place.

ASSEMBLY HALL STRUCK BY LIGHTNING. — During a severe thunderstorm on April 28th the Assembly Hall was struck and set on fire by lightning. The damage was not extensive.

CENSUS OF EDINBURGH. — The 1851 census was taken during May. The returns were: Edinburgh (royalty) 66,914, Edinburgh (St Cuthbert's and Canongate) 93,713, Leith 30,676, making a total of 191,303, an increase from 1841 of 27,131.

EX-QUEEN OF FRANCE VISITS EDINBURGH. — On July 8th the Countess of Neuilly and members of the ex-royal family of France arrived in Edinburgh, where they spent several days in sight-seeing.

1852

WELLINGTON STATUE. — On 14th June the Wellington statue was set up opposite the Register House. The unveiling took place with great pomp on 18th June, the anniversary of Waterloo.

LEITH DOCK. — On 17th August the Victoria Dock was opened at Leith for admission of vessels.

1853

THEATRE BURNED. — The Adelphi Theatre, situated in Broughton Street, was burnt to the ground on May 24th. Part of St Mary's Roman Catholic Chapel was also destroyed.

1854

FALL OF THE OLD CITY WALL. — A disaster occurred, through which several people lost their lives, in Leith Wynd, a narrow street with high tenement houses on one side and the city wall on the other. On February 22nd a large portion of the wall, which was 20 feet high and from 3 to 4 feet thick, gave way, and, with the embankment against which it was built, fell into the wynd. All who were in the wynd at the time of the accident were buried in the debris. Several days later 150 feet of the wall north of the portion which fell was removed by order of the Dean of Guild.

ADDITION TO HOLYROOD GROUNDS. — On March 9th, Her Majesty's Board of Works purchased the mansion-house and grounds of Croft-an-Righ with the intention of adding them to the grounds of Holyrood.

STATUE. — The statue of James Watt was placed in Adam Square and unveiled on May 12th.

NEW POST OFFICE. — On September 21st the Theatre-Royal, Shakespeare Square, and adjacent buildings, were bought with a view to erecting a new post office on the site.

1855

FREEDOM OF THE CITY. — On March 3rd Lord Nasmyth, in recognition of services at Silistria, Alma, and Balaclava, was presented with the freedom of the city.

LORD JEFFREY'S STATUE. — Steell's statue of Lord Jeffrey placed and unveiled in Parliament Hall on April 28th.

RIOT IN MEADOWS. — On 5th September Mr R F Gourlay, whose plans for the improvement of Edinburgh had been before the public for a considerable time, headed a mob and marched to the Meadows where they destroyed the stone pillars at the entrance which had been placed to prevent vehicular traffic.

NEW THEATRE FOR EDINBURGH. — On 19th December the Queen's Theatre and Opera House was opened.

1856

SOLDIERS' RETURN. — The return from the Crimea, in July, of the 92nd (Gordon) Highlanders and the 5th Dragoon Guards evoked great enthusiasm in the city. On the 31st of October the soldiers were entertained to a banquet in the Corn Exchange.

FALL OF GREYFRIARS' WALL. — From forty to fifty feet of the wall of Greyfriars' burying-ground fell on September 9th, immediately after a flash of lightning.

NEW CARRIAGE-WAY. — In the latter part of the year a new road was constructed from the Queen's Drive round Samson's Ribs and Windy Gowl to Portobello.

1857

OLD GREYFRIARS CHURCH. — On June 14th Old Greyfriars Church was re-opened, after total destruction by fire in 1845.

SENSATIONAL TRIAL. — June-July. — Sensational trial in the High Court of Madeleine Smith for the murder of Pierre L'Angelier, lasting nine days.

GREAT FIRE. — August 15th, a nine-story tenement at the top of the Mound (North Bank Street) was gutted by fire. Many exciting scenes of rescue. About a hundred people were rendered homeless. Here David Hume, historian, resided; also James Boswell of Auchinleck, who entertained Dr Johnson.

DR. LIVINGSTONE. — On September 21st the freedom of the city was presented to Dr. Livingstone, the distinguished missionary and African traveller.

THE MELVILLE MONUMENT. — On October 30th the statue of Lord Melville was placed in the centre of the new 'Place', west end of Melville Street.

1859

NEW ROAD. — The new drive through the Meadows was formally opened on January 25th, and was called after the then Lord Provost, viz Melville Drive.

THE FREEMASONS HALL. — The new hall in George Street of the Grand Lodge of Scotland was opened with masonic ceremonies on 24th February by His Grace the Duke of Atholl.

NATIONAL GALLERY. — On the 22nd March the National Gallery was opened to the public.

THE VOLUNTEERS. — During the month of May the Edinburgh Volunteer Rifle Corps was started.

THE PRINCE OF WALES. — On July 16th the Prince of Wales arrived in Edinburgh for the purpose of study. He remained until the 10th September.

NATIONAL MUSEUM OF ANTIQUITIES. — The National Museum of Antiquities wa inaugurated on December 23rd, under the presidency of Lord Neaves, and was opened to the public the following week.

1866

FALL OF A HOUSE IN HIGH STREET. — Part of a house at Bishop's Land, 129 High Street, fell on 30th January. Sixty-six people were dislodged by the accident, but no lives were lost.

1867

GREYFRIARS' INNOVATION CASE. — In March of this year proceedings were begun in the Presbytery of Edinburgh against Dr Robert Lee, minister of Old Greyfriars', for introducing a Service-book into that church. The Doctor, worn out with the controversy in the Church Courts, died the following March.

1870

CHAMBERS STREET. — In the course of the summer North College Street, Brown Square, and Adam Square were cleared away in order to make a new thoroughfare between the South Bridge and George IV Bridge, to be called Chambers Street.

ANNUITY TAX ABOLITION ACT. — After a second agitation, which began in 1860, and lasted ten years, the Annuity Tax Abolition Act was passed 10th August. Under this Act the Corporation paid over for the benefit of the City and Canongate clergy £56,500 in lieu of the obnoxious tax.

NEW RAILWAY STATION. — A new Caledonian Railway Station was opened on May 2nd at the west end of Princes Street.

FIRE. — The Britannia Flour Mills, Water of Leith, were destroyed by fire on August 5th. The damage was estimated at £10,000.

1873

THE EDINBURGH SCHOOL BOARD. — The first Edinburgh School Board was elected under Lord Advocate Young's Education Act of 1872 on 29th March. At the end of May 1875 the number of schools under the management of the Board was sixteen. The number of children on the roll at that time was 7142. The number of schools under the Board in June 1900 was thirty-one, and the number of children on the roll 37,923 — 22,350 boys and 15,573 girls. The total amount expended by the Board in building schools from the time it was established until 15th May 1900 was £529,510.

1881

SHOOTING OUTRAGES. — A series of shooting outrages took place in Edinburgh and Leith by two ruffians, Frederick Seymour, an Irish American, and James Grant, an Australian. Rather than allow himself to be apprehended, one of them shot himself dead.

DEATH OF CARLYLE. — This famous Scotsman died in London, 5th February 1881. By his will he bequeathed the estate of Craigenputtock to the University to found 'John Welsh' bursaries in the Arts Faculty in honour of his wife's fore-fathers.

1884

SCOTTISH AFFAIRS IN PARLIAMENT. — A great national meeting was held in the Free Assembly Hall, on 16th

January, in favour of the establishment of an independent Department, and the appointment of a responsible minister of State for the conduct of Scottish affairs. The Marquis of Lothian presided.

DOUBLE EXECUTION. — Innes and Vickers, Gorebridge miners, for the murder of a gamekeeper at Rosebery, were executed in the Calton Jail, 31st March.

BLACKFORD HILL. — This hill, on the south side of Edinburgh, was acquired in April as a public park for the city.

THEATRE ROYAL BURNED. — The Theatre Royal was totally destroyed by fire, 30th June.

SUBURBAN RAILWAY. — This railway was opened 16th October. It cost £225,000.

1889

HERIOT-WATT COLLEGE. — This college as extended was inaugurated, 10th January, by an address from Sir Frederick Bramwell.

EARTHQUAKE. — Another earthquake shock was experienced along the Water of Leith valley, 18th January.

EXECUTION. — Jessie King, Stockbridge, a baby farmer, for the murder of two children, was executed, 11th March, in the Calton Jail.

OPENING OF BRAID HILLS. — The formal opening of the Braid Hills to the public took place 29th May.

NAVAL AND MILITARY EXHIBITION. — An exhibition of

naval and military memorials was opened in the R.S.A. Galleries, 18th June.

SCOTTISH NATIONAL PORTRAIT GALLERY. — This building in Queen Street, gifted to the nation by Mr J R Findlay, of the *Scotsman*, was opened 15th July, by the Marquis of Lothian, Secretary for Scotland.

1890

FORTH BRIDGE. — Amid great enthusiasm the Prince of Wales, on 4th March, drove the last rivet into the Forth Bridge, and declared the Bridge open.

INTERNATIONAL EXHIBITION. — On 1st May the Duke of Edinburgh performed the opening ceremony at the Edinburgh International Exposition of Electrical Engineering, General Invention, and Industries at Colinton Road. The Lord Mayor of London visited the Exhibition in state, 20th June. The Exhibition was not a financial success, and the guarantors were called to pay the deficit.

PUBLIC LIBRARY. — On June 9th, the Public Library was opened by Lord Rosebery.

FIRE. — The Caledonian Station was, on June 16th, destroyed by fire.

1891

ST BERNARD'S WELL. — The re-opening of St Bernard's Well after the restoration of the mineral springs took place in April.

THE CHAMBERS STATUE. — This statue, erected in Chambers Street, was unveiled 5th March.

POPULATION. — The census taken this year gave the population of Edinburgh at 269,407 — males, 122,921; females, 146,486. Included in these figures is the population of Portobello, 8182.

FIRE. — On 12th October, the premises of Andrew Whyte and Sons, stationers, in Easter Road, were destroyed by fire, and damage done to the extent of £30,000.

BARNTON RAILWAY. — On 29th October the first sod of the Barnton Railway was cut.

1892

NEW CHURCHES. — On 18th May the Lord High Commissioner, the Marquis of Tweeddale, laid the foundation-stone of St Cuthbert's new Parish Church. The foundation-stone of the John Ker Memorial United Presbyterian Church, Polwarth Gardens, was laid on November 5th.

MUNICIPALISATION OF THE TRAMWAYS. — The Corporation as from 29th June resolved to acquire the street tramways. The price paid for the Edinburgh sections was £212,979.

PRINCESS LOUISE IN EDINBURGH. — On the forenoon of 18th October, the Princess Louise opened the Parliament Hall, which had been restored by Mr W Nelson, and in the afternoon she presented the Argyll and Sutherland Highlanders, then stationed at the Castle, with new colours.

NEW MUSIC HALL. - The Empire Palace Theatre of Varieties was opened on November 7th.

GREAT FIRE. — On November 26th, the premises of Messrs Charles Jenner and Company, silk mercers and drapers, were completely destroyed by fire. The damage was estimated at £250,000.

1893. MEMORIAL STATUE. — In the Old Calton Burying-ground a statue was unveiled on 21st August in memory of the Scottish-American soldiers who took part in the American Civil War.

1893

ROYAL VISITORS. — On October 2nd the Duke and Duchess of York visited Edinburgh to receive their wedding gift from the town. The presentation, which consisted of a service of glass for the table and a number of books, was made on the 3rd. The same day the Duke of York received the freedom of the city, and opened a new wing of the Longmore Hospital.

1894

SMALLPOX IN EDINBURGH . — There was an alarming smallpox scare in Edinburgh during May and the summer months. In July a temporary wooden hospital had to be erected in Queen's Park to relieve the other hospital. As many as seventy-six cases occurred during the week ending 23rd June.

CRAIG HOUSE ASYLUM. — On 26th October the new Craig House Asylum was opened, in presence of a large company, by the Duke and Duchess of Buccleuch.

THE LORD PROVOST. — Mr Andrew McDonald was elected Lord Provost after the November elections. The figures were: McDonald, 21; Sir James Russell, 20.

1895

DEATH OF PROFESSOR BLACKIE. — On 2nd March the death occurred of Professor Blackie. An imposing funeral, with an escort of pipers, took place on 6th March from St Giles' Cathedral to the Dean Cemetery.

ELECTRIC LIGHTING OF EDINBURGH. — The electric light — installed at a cost of about £120,000 — was turned on in the city on 11th April for the first time by Mrs McDonald, wife of the Lord Provost.

HONOUR TO LORD HOPETOUN. — Lord Hopetoun, in recognition of his eminent services as Governor of Victoria, was entertained on his return to a banquet in the Waterloo Hotel on 6th June. Over 230 gentlemen were present, presided over by Lord Provost McDonald. In presence of a large gathering, on 10th July in the Music Hall, the freedom of the city was conferred on the Earl of Hopetoun.

EDINBURGH'S NEW WATER-WORKS. — The ceremony of cutting the first sod of the new Talla water-works was performed by Mrs McDonald on 28th September at Tweedsmuir, on the south bank of the Tweed.

SOUTH AFRICANS IN TOWN. — King Khama and his freinds, Sebele and Bathoen, were entertained to tea in the City Chambers on 23rd October.

1896

EXTENSION BILL. — An important Act was passed through Parliament this summer, under which Portobello was taken into the city, and the boundaries otherwise extenxded. An amlgamation was sought to be effected with Leith, but that part opposed by Leith was thrown out by Parliament.

OBSERVATORY. — On April 7th a new observatory, which had taken four years to erect, was opened on Blackford Hill.

KNOX STATUE. — A statue im memory of John Knox was unveiled in the quadrangle of the Free Church College on 22nd May.

NEW NORTH BRIDGE. — On 25th May Lord Provost McDonald laid the foundation-stone of the new North Bridge.

FRANCO-SCOTTISH SOCIETY. — This Society opened a week's series of meetings, 12th July.

1897

BUTCHERS' BOYCOTT. — Great discussion took place in consequence of the butchers in Glasgow and Edinburgh endeavouring to prevent Co-operative Societies purchasing at public sales cattle for slaughter. The butchers were unsuccessful in permanently maintaining the boycott.

MASONS' STRIKE. — A strike of masons took place August 2nd, in Edinburgh and Leith for an eight-hours day.

NEW NORTH BRIDGE. — Lord Provost Sir Andrew McDonald opened the new North Bridge 15th September. The bridge consists of three girder spans of 175 feet each. It is 75 feet wide, and cost £90,000, of which £30,000 was contributed by the North British Railway Company.

MR W McEWAN, M.P. — The freedom of the city was presented, 22nd October, to Mr W McEwan, M.P., in recognition of his munificence to the University.

NEW LORD PROVOST. — Mr Mitchell Thomson was on 5th November elected Lord Provost. His opponents were Mr Kinloch Anderson and Treasurer McCrae. In the final vote Mr Mitchell Thomson was elected as against Treasurer McCrae by the casting vote of the chairman, Bailie Sloan.

TRAGEDY IN THE POLICE OFFICE. — Teresa Ulfield, supposed at first to have been a Russian countess, shot herself, 16th November, in the Police Office, where she had been asked to call in connection with an inquiry concerning the loss of her purse.

PROFESSOR MASSON. — In connection with his retirement from the Chair of Rhetoric, Professor Masson was presented with his portrait and bust, the latter being intended for the University.

DEATH OF PROFESSOR CALDERWOOD. — Dr Henry Calderwood, Professor of Moral Philosophy, Edinburgh University, died suddenly, 19th November.

THE McEWAN HALL. — The McEwan Hall, New University, erected from designs by Dr Rowand Anderson, at a cost of £110,000, defrayed by Mr McEwan, M.P., was opened December 3rd by Mr A J Balfour, M.P., the Chancellor. The honorary degree of LL.D. was conferred on the donor. The inaugural concert took place of the 14th December, at which Madame Ella Russell was the principal vocalist.

1898

NORTH BRIDGE STREET. — The Town Council agreed, 17th January, to expose the cleared areas on the east and west sides of North Bridge Street for £230,000 at a sale on 13th March. The west side was purchased for £120,000 by the *Scotsman* proprietors, and the stance at the south-east end by the Commercial Bank for £35,000. The middle and north sections on the east side remained at that time unsold.

EXECUTION. — John Herdman, printer, for the murder of a woman in Milne's Square on 21st February, was executed in the Calton Jail, 14th March.

SCAFFOLDING ACCIDENT. — A huge scaffolding, erected to support a crane on the top of the North British Railway new hotel, fell in a gale of wind, 18th March. Two workmen were killed and thirteen injured.

1900

CAR EXHIBITION. — An exhibition of motor cars, which had arrived in Edinburgh after the first half of a thousand miles run, took place 3rd May.